D1142383

TUNNEL VISIONS

TUNNEL VISIONS

Journeys of an Underground Philosopher

Christopher Ross

FOURTH ESTATE • *London*

First published in Great Britain in 2001 by
Fourth Estate
A Division of HarperCollins*Publishers*
77–85 Fulham Palace Road,
London W6 8JB
www.4thestate.co.uk

10 9 8 7 6 5 4 3 2

A catalogue record for this book is available from the
British Library.

ISBN 1-84115-566-7

Typeset by Rowland Phototypesetting Limited,
Bury St Edmunds, Suffolk.
Printed in Great Britain by
Clays Ltd, St Ives plc

This book is dedicated to all those
without whom it could not
have been written

Contents

PART I

Into the Tunnel

1

PART II

Tunnel Visions

55

PART III

Imbrications

135

PART IV

Light at the End

163

Invitation to Travellers:

sequi me

The use of travelling is to
regulate imagination by reality, and
instead of thinking how things may be,
to see them as they are.

SAMUEL JOHNSON

PART I

Into the Tunnel

It seemed that out of battle I escaped
Down some profound dull tunnel, long
since scooped
Through granites which titanic wars
had groined.

'STRANGE MEETING', WILFRED OWEN

(1)

I waited for the expected question. *When are you going home?*

Other questions preceded it. When had I arrived in the country? Was I was working or studying, or perhaps a tourist? But it was conventional to conclude such formalities with a third and final enquiry. Always the same one. *When are you going home?*

After only a short time in the country I began to notice conversations assumed a predictable pattern. Of course, there were conventional answers to conventional questions. They caused little trouble, like dance steps once learned, both parties knowing how to avoid colliding or treading on each other's toes.

When are you going home? was a question I wrestled with in the quieter moments, whenever I considered my life and the direction it seemed to be taking. Conventions were useless when you were both the questioner and the questioned. For nearly ten years I had lived in a dozen countries. And I had travelled through dozens more; usually in pursuit of a purpose or a person; occasionally to see the sights.

This kind of travel – not aimless wandering, but extensive exploration of a wide variety of cultures – doesn't allow the putting down of roots. Unlike business travel where hotel chains and office buildings all begin to look alike, the peregrinations of the independently minded disorientate because *nothing* remains the same. It's a flux. A kaleidoscope. And the moment you find your bearings it's time to move on – once again to face the task of understanding a new world bravely.

At the back of your mind, like a faint memory, is

the idea of home. Of the place you came from. Of your origins. Of return.

After ten years in the Far East, the Near East, the East; time spent in Australia and the Americas and sorties into Africa and improbable parts of Europe, I flew home. What now?

(2)

Cease to be ruled by dogmas and authorities; look at the world! declared Roger Bacon in the thirteenth century. Seven hundred years later I was struggling to come to terms with this, an invitation to a life of revolutionary travail. But my fight was personal, not political; my view philosophical, not strictly practical. I was a wanderer and, I hoped, a thinking man, who had lived away from the land of his birth to see things from other perspectives.

For a decade I followed no career path, simply doing whatever was required in any country I happened to be in to earn enough to live on, with something left over to journey on to the next halting place, moving whenever it seemed necessary or appropriate. I sometimes characterised myself as a nomad, but knew that this was a mild conceit; a nomad moves to ensure his livestock can eat fresh pasture, or to guarantee good hunting, not to see the world and meet its peoples. But the term sometimes seemed good enough to distinguish me from the majority of mankind, for whom a permanent home, a fixed place about which to turn, is a priority. And the sense that nomads were outside all contemporary societies, except their own, answered to something in me, something unformulated but essential.

I once had a career which seemed to be going well

and where I earned more money than was perhaps good for a young man. Feeling sure of myself and the quickness of my mind, it seemed material rewards were mine by right; I could easily see the connection between the work I did and large sums flowing into the company which employed me. Had I continued in this way, I am sure, I would have had a life of ease, free of money worries, and steadily accruing a measure of respect for my person and status. I have no doubt now that I would have fallen victim to the 'cleverness trap', in which you are intelligent only in your own interest and lack soul. Who knows, eventually I might have decided to impose myself on others as completely as I could manage. I might have become a politician, an activist in some cause or other or perhaps a magistrate, unwittingly working steadily to corrode my real self beyond repair, to fuse the connections to my real being and join the living dead, whom, significantly, we permit to rule over us.

I met someone whom I came to accept as a mentor, although at that time I was foolish enough to think I didn't need a teacher. Although he is no longer alive as I write this, for me he lives on in every significant sense and I am able to re-orientate myself by reflecting on what he said and did, by what he was, whenever I go too far in the wrong direction. One of the first things he told me, when I was twenty-one, was that *no one ever lost their way on a straight path*. Later I identified this as a quotation, also taken from the thirteenth century, from the wanderer and sage Sheikh Saadi of Shiraz and echoed by Dante: 'I woke to find myself in a dark wood, for I had wandered off from the straight path' (*Inferno*, Canto I).

I did not then know what a straight path might look like in the confusion and complexity of the modern world, but was convinced that the route I was travelling was twisted and appeared to be twisting further at an alarming pace. Perhaps it was time to simplify things. *What are the essentials for a considered life and what may be discarded?* Making any progress with this question took time and, unsurprisingly, it is something I am still working on. It is partly what this small book is about.

At twenty-six I abandoned my employed life and began to travel widely. The particular places were more or less randomly selected, or arose out of day to day circumstances. But my decision to live outside my own culture was a conscious choice. I had provisionally accepted the wisdom of Kipling's *No man knows England, who only England knows*. It was simply not enough to participate in your own culture in order to understand it; but like a fish out of water, by moving outside what I had always taken for granted, I came to recognise its value. And it was necessary actually to experience the loss. Imagining it would not do.

I was, furthermore, seeking not only to broaden my mind, to expand the spectrum of my way of thinking, but also to experience the specialisations of other cultures, which I thought of as *ways of seeing*, subtleties having little or nothing to do with the obvious differences: chopsticks versus knives and forks, variations in idioms. The nuances I sought involved faculties beyond those presumed necessary – like television, a sound and vision medium, catering for an extra sense, such as the sense of smell, and in this way providing the missing piece of the puzzle, a piece which brings everything else into a clearer focus, a truer perspective.

In practical terms, of course, what my life in foreign climes meant on a daily basis was usually not at all dramatic. It involved all the mundane things – eating, sleeping, chores, work and distractions. Most of the time it was the opposite of dramatic, and it would be imprudent to write truthfully and fully about what I did, said and saw, as such an account could not hope to hold any normal reader's attention. What matters though, is what I learned from my travels. Lessons that might prove useful to anyone facing similar doubts about their lives: what, having undergone the experiences of this period, resulted; how it changed me; and what general truths or hints for living (if any!) may be gleaned from sifting through my recollections of this phase. Additionally, from time to time, as with most lives, there were crises and dramatic interludes and I shall describe some of them where they serve to tell part of the meaning of my story.

However, even an action-packed and eventful life is mostly a succession of nothings, of things we cannot and do not notice, because we perceive them hardly at all. This realisation caused me to become very interested in the idea of heightening focus on the ordinary, of looking hard, or in another way, during the undramatic interludes to see if indeed 'nothing is happening', or, as I suspected, whether this is a perceptual deception. The best way to do this, I reasoned, would be to do something fairly mechanical over a long enough period to wear out the novelty effects; something not too challenging so as to free up enough energy and attention to perform the experiment well. How would a questing mind cope with a dull and lacklustre life of toil in some under-appreciated corner? Years were to pass – and by then I had returned to England – before I had an opportunity to revive my interest in this question. What happens when *nothing* is happening?

(3)

According to some anthropologists, among the
least technologically developed societies, such as the
tribesmen of the Brazilian jungles or the African deserts,
grown men rarely spend more than four hours a
day providing for their livelihood – the rest of the time
they spend resting, chatting, singing and dancing.
MIHALY CSIKSZENTMIHALYI

I walk up and down, in a confined yet high-ceilinged space, about 100 feet under ground, stopping from time to time to answer questions. My workaday world, never far from Platform 6 at Oxford Circus Station, from 7.30 in the morning until half past eleven. Only four hours of work each weekday, just twenty hours a week. An ugly uniform *fashioned* from man-made fibres and a glowing, 3M Scotchlite™ orange hi-visibility vest advertise my function: I am there to serve the travelling public.

In another sense I was there because I was broke and had, I felt, hardly any energy available to allocate to earning a living. This was not because I was worn out, I simply had too many other interests, none of which I would give up, activities which yielded no income. Money had to be considered and so I was there because I needed a job and it would do. Any routine and remunerative task which absorbed the time I could spare would do. Start early, finish early was my strategy. Time I would otherwise spend asleep seemed ideal; it was deadtime not dreamtime, for I never remembered my dreams and felt sure I could catch up on being dead later on.

This was a pattern which seemed to suit my approach

to life. Work at something, anything, accumulate some savings and then stop working and do something more rewarding. I refused to think too hard about how long I could keep this up – I had always managed to maintain a sense of progress, despite various hardships met over the years, and felt confident that whenever I was really needy something would turn up. So far I had been right.

Money I saved in Japan lasted a year, but eventually ran out. I was in London and, needing a job, answered an advertisement to see if I qualified to work, part-time, as a Station Assistant, or SA, on the London Underground, an institution I had always thought of as the Tube. My confidence was not high as I had been turned down as a street sweeper the week before, 'We think you're a little over-qualified,' they'd said on the telephone without knowing anything about me.

I decided to persist and try to find something part-time in the blue-collar category. Work for my body, something that could quickly be mastered, leaving my mind free. Body work, not body and soul work. Even typing in an office was, I thought, likely to occupy too much of any available energy and attention. And there seemed to be a money correlation; more than a certain amount an hour and you were 'owned' by your employer, both in his mind and, perhaps more importantly, in your own.

During the pre-interview screening, and the first and second interviews, I smiled a lot and told the necessary lies to convince anyone I encountered that I really, *really* wanted to go down the Tubes: 'It is my ideal part-time job,' I dissimulated. I had to mind the truth gap as any truthful account of my most recent employments – oriental carpet smuggler in Dubai; camel cowboy in the

Australian outback; Jesuit priest in a daytime Japanese television soap whose followers are captured one by one and crucified – would not do. Sometimes the truth is, quite simply, unbelievable.

(4)

We are confused about the subject of lying. We all lie many times a day and yet, were we to be questioned, I am sure most of us would claim to tell the truth 'most of the time'. A simplistic approach does not lead very far – it is not very helpful to state lying is bad and telling the truth good, when it is easy to imagine situations where the opposite seems to hold. It is helpful to distinguish several kinds of lying and to classify lying in a number of useful ways. One division is to separate lying consciously or deliberately from lying automatically or as a reflex reaction. The significance of this classification is the capacity to control behaviour – and rather than premeditation making matters worse, it is better to lie consciously than without volitional control. The fact is, you cannot choose truth until you can choose; choice means departing from being operated by compulsions, reflexes and reactions.

This leads on to the next classification: that of the effect and purpose of lying. There are only a few terms in English to qualify a lie by purpose, the best known of which is the white lie. In other languages there are terms which reveal a much greater degree of sophistication. There are verbs which mean 'lying to conceal a benefit you have conferred on another', 'lying to show that someone lacks perception and may be a fool', and 'lying to be seen to lie and in this way to confuse'. It is worth spelling out the base idea: the effect of telling the truth is not always good or beneficial; the effect of lying is not always bad or harmful. In consequence we may regard lying as an instrument, neutral in itself, like a knife; and like a knife it may be used for good or ill according to the capacity and skill and the nature of the person employing it.

(5)

A moment's reflection confirmed there was simply no room for the facts. Another thing I planned not to reveal to the Tube recruiters was that I no longer thought in terms of a career. Money was just the means to the freedom necessary to continue my search. I was seeking something far more durable, was in search of the truth; by increments, I had become a philosopher. I do not mean a philosopher in the western modern academic tradition – an arena which often seems devoid of contemporary and practical relevance to most non-philosophers. My approach was not to seek initiation into a private world, alien and inaccessible to ordinary people; I was concerned with questions which had, I believed, very great relevance to all. Practical concerns: how might we best behave in various situations? How should we use our time? What duties, if any, were ours to fulfil? How can we say we know anything? Can we discover the purpose and potential of our lives?

(6)

What, indeed, is a philosopher?

Imagine a surface, grey and striated, like the moon. Panning back a little we realise it is less like rock than skin. Further back still, we understand it is the skin of an animal. Retreating further reveals that it is a large animal – is it a rhino? or a hippopotamus? Fully back now we see, clearly and for the first time, that we have been looking at an elephant. Knowledge of elephants confirms it is an Indian elephant.

Everything is perceptually modified by proximity and perspective and philosophy is the capacity to pan in and out at will – and a philosopher is someone who can do this.

(7)

I realised my philosophical orientation might seem anachronistic or a fool's errand, but it seemed right for me. It was a path without any obvious form or visible destination, only a method. The method was to seek. To try to see what is real, what matters, to discover why people do what they do. I was searching for meaning or, put another way, was learning to see.

I wouldn't mention that to my new employers either.

(8)

The Training Department was administered from the eighth floor, but on the first day we were to gather in a lounge on the second floor reached by stairs or by only some of the lifts. The other lifts were programmed to stop on certain important floors only, such as the ninth which housed the subsidised canteen and the smoking room.

It was clear from a quick scan of the amorphous crowd milling around in the second-floor lounge that not everyone was new; some dressed in worn and faded uniforms were obviously experienced staff attending refresher courses and some told me they had, in a burst of ambition, decided to become train drivers.

(9)

I was interested to learn that the drivers of trains on lines operating automatically – such as the Central and Victoria lines – are not driving the trains at all. They sit at the front and open and close the doors. They engage and disengage the automatic system, but the trains are driven by computers located far from the driver's cab. Experiments with dummies and empty driver's cabs revealed that passengers were uncomfortable with fully automatic trains and preferred the illusion of someone sitting up front, seemingly in control.

(10)

The new recruits were divided into three groups and there were also three trainers, one for each group. I was assigned to Elizabeth's group, the only woman trainer and in her early forties I guessed as she smiled and said something mild and self-effacing. Fine, I thought. I liked her smiling face, her unfussy clothes.

We were led down a corridor. All the classrooms were named for English generals and statesmen. We were in Churchill, another group next door in Marlborough. We sat down at random and wrote our names on a cardboard sign with brand-new marker pens that induce nausea in confined spaces, the kind manufactured in Seoul and printed with a health warning in *Hangul*. I toyed with writing 'Mr Ross', something of the classroom environment forcing me into a rebellious frame of mind, but thought better of it and instead wrote 'Chris'. There were nine others apart from me and Elizabeth the trainer in Churchill. Five men and four women. Four of us were black, two ethnically Asian and four, including me, were white. Elizabeth was also Caucasian.

After we had written our names and received a huge white ring-binder dauntingly full of pages, Elizabeth asked us to introduce ourselves. I volunteered to go first to break the ice. I said I had just returned from the Cannes Film Festival – which was true – practised martial arts – which was also true – and was looking forward to working for London Underground in order to meet and help a wide variety of people – a lie. Or was it?

Elizabeth pressed me to elaborate: why was I at the Cannes Film Festival? which martial arts did I practise? She ignored my professed desire to help people. I explained I had been living in France, near Nice, to continue studying the Japanese martial art of aikido, which I'd taken up in Japan. A famous western expert, though a long-term resident of Japan, now lived in Valbonne working for a Japanese/French hi-tech joint venture and I was his student. I also practised iaido, the art of sword drawing. Samurai quick draw, one cut one life. When I said this, Elizabeth smiled and frowned in quick succession and took an exaggerated step back in mock fear, as if I might have a sword hidden in my clothes. As if I might take her life with just one, sudden, cut.

(11)

I stood in the long grass a short distance from my tent breathing slow, regular breaths. A dawn mist was drifting near the surface of the Loire in the direction I faced. Behind me there was a main road. I had camped on the verge separating the main road from a place where trucks could stop or turn around. There was nothing much to note, except discarded beer cans and empty bottles to indicate others had passed before me.

I raised the wooden sword and cut, raised it again and cut again. I kept it up, building a rhythm, trying to relax my shoulders and to use the weight of the sword, swinging it out in an arc which ended a fist's length from my belly, the hara, or stomach-centre so important in the Japanese martial arts. The hara is the centre of your being, the seat of the soul.

I was practising suburi, an iaido exercise also used in aikido, as a way of waking up and reviving stiff muscles. Stripped to the waist, swinging a wooden sword, a puzzling sight I supposed for the passing lorry drivers, but I didn't think about that, just cut, breathe, relax, eyes focused on the sun rising above the mist-shrouded river.

(12)

I didn't want to try to explain what martial arts meant to me in this brief introduction and wondered as soon as I'd mentioned it if it would have been better to make something up. Something else, something that meant nothing, for wasn't information a form of power? Was I trusting Elizabeth with something of value as a kind of exchange, hoping in return to receive her goodwill, good grades and, in the end, the job I really needed?

Elizabeth went round the class, encouraging and flattering, working her audience like a warm-up man for a live TV situation comedy show. She smiled all the time and her body language seemed lifted straight out of the pages of Desmond Morris, expertly designed to put us at our collective ease. In between each account she told jokes against herself, made unfavourable comparisons: whatever the last speaker could do, she could not. We knew what it meant, what it was for and didn't take it at face value. It was unlikely, after all, that we were to be taught by a complete idiot, no good at sport or at school work, from a broken home and whose life was a trail of wrecked and tragic relationships.

In Elizabeth's eyes, everyone seemed to be a star. Dan, who had just graduated from the Slade School of Fine Art, was working to save up for his own studio and played the bongos when not painting. Elizabeth offered to buy one of his paintings, sight unseen. Dexter, a cool dude black boy, wasn't the rap singer he appeared to be, but a medical student at Charing Cross. Elizabeth admired the elaborate way he had decorated his cardboard name card. Aalapi was congratulated on the beauty of her exotic name and that she was studying to be a solicitor. Trish, a large kind-faced woman who worked part-time at Heathrow Airport in the Disney theme shop, revealed she was close to finishing her degree in aeronautical engineering. 'Wow!' said Elizabeth, 'a rocket scientist!' Shaz, a good-looking boy with a naughty grin, played county cricket and was in between degrees, but soon to start a master's in business studies. In his spare time he did kickboxing.

The others all acquitted themselves equally well, if not academically then because of their hobbies or previous jobs, until it was Judith's turn to speak. Judith, a quicksilver black cockney in an outsized Tommy Hilfiger T-shirt, belted and worn as a summer dress, complained she hadn't done anything and in this company felt stupid. 'Don't be silly,' said Elizabeth, who probed and sifted and after a couple of questions discovered that Judith was a single parent, had a nine-month-old little boy. We passed his photo around and Judith's pretty baby drew forth formulaic, but not insincere, baby picture approval noises. 'See,' said Elizabeth, 'having a baby is a *real* achievement.' Judith looked unconvinced. 'You saying I'm good at *shagging*?'

(13)

I had no idea what Elizabeth's subject, Soft Skills, would involve. Social sciences I guessed. Pop psychology filleted and applied to produce happy workers in an ever more efficient enterprise, joyously interfacing with optimistic and sated customers who just couldn't get enough of our services. Something like that.

Elizabeth began to explain that she would take us through London Underground's Customer Care programme, a fairly new initiative, Dealing with Complaints and, for those of us who proved no good at dealing with complaints, Assault Awareness. Shaz the Kickboxer's eyes lit up. 'Yeah,' he said, cracking the knuckles of both hands all at once, '*hard* skills!'

In the mid-morning break we fell on the free coffee

and biscuits laid out in the lounge area like prep-school boys let loose on the Parents' Tea on Sports Day. I like good coffee and correspondingly find bad coffee un-drinkable. The free stuff was brown water and I decided to chance some small change on a heavily subsidised vending-machine espresso.

Three people ahead of me in the queue for the machine struggled with their drinks as they extracted hot, over-full cardboard cups. A design fault made spilling your drink a likelihood. When it was my turn I called to mind Saadi's dictum, *Learn from the mistakes of others, so that they need not learn from yours,* and gingerly lifted the cardboard cup of perfect Italian coffee which had fallen out of the machine, without spilling any.

Dexter, who was next, like me rejecting the free stuff, selected hot chocolate, and I explained how to remove the cup without spilling it and watched him spoon in five sugars. 'Sweet tooth?' I asked. 'Yeah, I need the sugar to stay awake, man. Was out till four this morning.' There was something of Alice's dormouse about Dexter. Staying awake long enough to finish his sentences seemed an almighty struggle. At the same time he managed to convey how dull he found the prospect of three weeks of pointless study, as everyone we had questioned said how nothing you learned at the Training Centre was of the slightest use when you were working on a station. 'Like medicine,' I said, 'not much of what you learn stays with you. It's a rite of passage. You know, like circumcision without flinching or spearing your first lion alone.' I wondered if Dexter would react to my African examples, but he seemed to have fallen asleep.

(14)

Why is it that even random groupings seem to solidify and resist change when faced with novel situations?

Despite Elizabeth's efforts to shuffle the pack, we would always take the first opportunity to rearrange in our original 4:3:3 configuration, as if finding our natural equilibrium or even a chemical stability. Ten people might be combined in any number of ways, but I noticed we sat in the same seats with the randomly chosen two or three others we had started out with. I was with Dexter, Dan and Shaz.

Dan, the artist, was blond and appeared younger than twenty-four. He had pink skin and rosy cheeks. He looked Californian until he smiled and you saw his less than perfect English teeth. Dan always spoke slowly, as if chewing his words and only reluctantly allowing them out of his mouth. The speed of his speech suggested an underlying slowness of mind; but this was an illusion.

Shaz, his own abbreviation for what he took to be his unpronounceable Pakistani name, was always smiling and was firmly in the grip of two obsessions: cricket and sex. I told him I knew next to nothing about cricket, so he naturally switched to girls, telling me one morning out of the blue as I nibbled a digestive biscuit that his favourite sex position was rear entry or doggy-style. 'Why?' I asked, although I was more interested in whether I could get back to the biscuit table in time for a second digestive before they were all gone. 'Because, then you don't have to kiss. I don't like kissing much. It's so unhygienic.'

(15)

Elizabeth asked us to read out the answers to the exercises she had set to highlight Customer Care concerns. She scored points on the board, but there was little feeling of competition and each group had amassed next to identical reasons to justify being careful with one's customers. One reason given by both the other groups, but not us, was 'It's more fun to be polite and helpful.' I knew what they meant, but suspected hypocrisy. It could, I imagined, be a lot more fun being spiteful, sarcastic and revengeful – as long as you had ceased to care.

(16)

Over lunch a group of us mumbled inconsequentially, making small talk, during which Elizabeth, who had joined our table, revealed she was the great-grandniece of Emilie Le Breton, the actress Lillie Langtry and mistress to King Edward VII. After the meal I excused myself and left the building for some fresh air. I often reflected on how few links separated me from well-known figures, testing the theory that there are only six degrees of separation between any two persons. In a superficial sense, as well as a real one, we are all closer to each other than we care to admit. But I had not expected a short link to a dead king. Not today.

(17)

Empathy is the capacity to put yourself into the position of another person; to feel what he feels, understand his situation by imagining it is your own situation. All wars involve the use of propaganda to de-humanise, to demonise, the enemy in order to make the act of killing more accessible to the ordinary person. It is designed to destroy empathy. Whenever we encounter someone disagreeable, it is worthwhile attempting an empathetic exercise: if this person has a fault, how much of it is in me too?

(18)

Training on trains, a trainer trains trainees. Training on trains, a trainer trains trainees, the rattling carriages seemed to whisper as I journeyed home. Each of these words, I knew, derived from the Latin *trahere*, 'to pull or draw along'. I was to spend three weeks being pulled in a particular direction, hitched, as it were, to a variety of locomotives and run down various well-worn tracks bordered with signals as to the significance of the scenery. At the end of each trip there would be questions about what I had seen – and only if my recall was good enough, orthodox enough, what was expected, would I be eligible for the next part of the journey.

(19)

I had often thought of my progress through life and the life of the mind, my ability to think, feel and understand, as a journey. It seemed germane that certain means of transport, such as the passenger car and even more so the train, could go only where road or rails had gone before them. Freedom to travel by such means then is only the freedom to choose between existing routes. No train traveller carries rails to lay down a new track as they go along, to blaze a trail. Other means of moving about, such as flight, require care to avoid collisions with other similarly free travellers, but in this they do not really differ from fixed route travellers, who seem to collide quite frequently. To walk across a plain, even up and down a mountain should it be in the way, is a fundamental and superior form of freedom, a freedom more or less unencumbered by means. But what of speed? Or unscalable obstacles? Of health and strength?

(20)

It felt like the middle of the night as I struggled awake and somnambulated my way to Training Centre. I had been told many times as a child that most great men and women were early risers, larks, presumably larks risen early to catch the proverbial worm. Whenever any-one spoke of early birds and worms I liked to counter-attack with a story of Mulla Nasrudin, the Middle Eastern wise-idiot joker:

> Mulla Nasrudin decided to bully his lazy son into recognising the benefits of rising early. 'Heh,' he said, 'look what I found early this morning when I went for a walk,' holding up a bag of gold. 'It just shows how getting up early is lucky.' 'How do you know it wasn't there the night before?' asked his still-sleepy son. 'I passed that way quite

late and it definitely wasn't there,' said the Mulla. 'Well,' said his son turning over in bed, 'being up early can't be lucky for everyone. What about the person who lost the gold? He must have been up even earlier than you!'

(21)

The canteen was empty. All the cooked breakfast items were displayed in stainless steel warming trays and everything smelled *exactly right*. I asked for two fried eggs, which were prepared on request, and pointed successively at a sausage, baked beans, a slice of black pudding, some mushrooms and two or three slices of back bacon – and then at the sausages again, in case one was not enough to assuage my greed. By the time my choices had been transferred on to a warm plate, the fried eggs were ready, and the two slices of toast I'd asked for popped up out of an industrial-sized toaster. I snatched up some pats of butter, helped myself to a large mug of filter coffee and slid the tray along to the cash register. One thing extensive travel had taught me – when you wake up tired and hungry, there is nothing so perfect as the perfectly cooked English breakfast.

(22)

I knelt on the platform, supporting a young woman who had suddenly slumped down in front of me as she stepped out of a packed Victoria Line train at 7.45 in the morning. A man stood near by, elderly and with a look of concern on his face. I asked the woman how she felt and ran through the by now standard questions for situations like this. No, she had not had time to eat breakfast. It had been very hot inside the train and she had found it hard to breathe. The woman was helped away by a first-aid-trained member of staff who had arrived with a glass of water, which we relied on as a sort of panacea. The elderly man spoke for the first time and told me he was a professor of medicine, a specialist in neurology.

'I believe the issue of breakfast may provide answers to a variety of important questions,' said the professor. 'Why do juveniles have mood swings? What is the relationship of energy to success? Can you get anywhere in life using chemical stimulants as a substitute for internally generated effort and self-discipline? To drink coffee or not to drink coffee, is one way to pose this question.' Here he paused, sliding his glasses back up his shiny nose. I nodded to indicate I was still paying attention.

'If man is an emotional being and if he has far less control over his emotional self than his so-called rational self, is it in this area we should search for the answers to perennial paradoxes of lifestyle restlessness and to explain curious behaviour? Why do we rush, like lemmings, over the cliff face of our own undoing so blindly and so often I ask you?' Here he paused, but did not seem to expect me to answer. 'My answer is not metaphysical, but physical: the balance of our minds is disturbed, which means, simply stated, that the chemicals in your brain are mixed in such a way as to provoke trouble. You are what you eat or – as in the case of our unfortunate fainting lady – what you don't eat.' At this he smiled and, seeming all of a sudden to remember he was going somewhere, turned around and walked away without another word.

In Tokyo I used to breakfast on a piece of salmon that had been brushed with thick, dark soy and grilled. It was served with miso soup, green beans and a bowl of rice. I liked to imagine where the fish had started its life, where it had swum, what it had seen of the dry world beyond its own wet environment, glimpsed through a watery filter. Did it ever consider its final destiny as . . . my breakfast?

Of all meals, breakfast is the meal one is least inclined to experiment with. Yet, when I have done so, as with the Japanese salmon start to the day, I am usually pleased, feeling a new horizon has dawned. I feel inspired to ask questions like the professor. Is breakfast a measure of cross-cultural tolerance: if I can stomach your breakfast, and only then, can I sincerely say we may live together without fear? Isn't this, perhaps, what the expression 'You're not my cup of tea' refers to? Only by participation in another culture may we accept it, and we may grant that breakfast is a benchmark, a moment when the duplicitous mind is still half asleep and when we are inclined to visceral, truthful, reactions.

(23)

We left Tehran in the middle of the night. I tried hard not to doze, as although my companion was an extremely safe driver we would be taking the martyrway and were travelling in a Paykan, the ubiquitous Hillman Hunter copy, with reconditioned tyres on three of the wheels. The martyrway was my name for the stretch of high-speed road which linked Tehran and the religious city of Qom. Along its length were displayed posters of those killed in the Islamic revolution and the war with

Iraq; there was a different face every four hundred metres or so and many were beautiful boys far too young to have died violent deaths. Last time we had come this way we had blown a tyre at 100 mph and had spun around and around, just missing a collision with a juggernaut loaded with watermelons. Exhaling with relief, I glimpsed the receding rows of green humps, as the lorry thundered past.

We arrived on the outskirts of Qom just as my eyelids had turned to lead. I began to doze as the car waited at some traffic lights, operating automatically in the dawn half light. A tapping on the glass of my door window brought me back from sleep and I turned to see my gaze returned by a bird; a golden eagle with its massive wings fully outstretched, hovering three feet or so off the ground and only inches from my face. It tapped again with its beak and only then did I notice the fingers wrapped around the middle of its body. The owner of the bird stood up, gesturing to enquire if we would like to buy it. What, I wondered, inspires anyone to attempt to sell stuffed birds of prey to early-morning motorists in the gloom of a Qom winter morning?

Declining the bird we pulled off the road for breakfast. *Haleem* is a wheat porridge and was served on this occasion topped with shredded lamb and brown sugar. My companion set about his bowl with relish, I forced some down, dreaming of hot buttered toast.

(24)

I finished off the last slice of toast and, taking the stairs, wandered slowly down to class. Despite being warned to be on time both Dexter and Shaz arrived late. They

had well-prepared defences and excused themselves
with detailed and sincere sounding apologies.

Mid-morning, in the coffee break, I sat alone next
to a window with a glass of water. Chemicals were still
buzzing inside me and I didn't want to add to the disagreeable drugged feeling by drinking yet more coffee.
I was musing about the question of offering excuses for
some shortfall in behaviour. In Japan I had learned a
lesson which I now felt was very important. Adults must
take responsibility for their own fate and should not
be encouraged to shift the blame, even when it might
otherwise seem reasonable to do so. Blame shifting leads
to a culture of victimhood.

A sort of tit-for-tat social system is used by the Japanese in their day-to-day relationships. It works on a don't
get mad, get even principle. If I am late by ten minutes
for an appointment to meet you, the next time we meet
you are late by the same number of minutes and so on.
Once the recompense has been exacted it is forgotten
and never again referred to, the offence which caused
it having been in this way cancelled. This kind of balanc-
ing is usually immediate and sometimes seems almost
automatic, rather than a calculated act of revenge timed
to exact retribution.

In the Japanese workplace excuses are listened
to, but essentially they are ignored. If you are absent or
late more than a certain number of times action will
follow to get rid of you, or prevent you from advancing
in the organisation. If you are responsible for a certain
project which fails, you will suffer, will be where the
buck stops. Others may have a mirrored failure; for,
having chosen you, they have in a sense guaranteed
that you will succeed, and, like ripples flowing from a
single stone dropped into a pool of water, will all have

to take responsibility according to the magnitude of the event.

(25)

After spending the previous day with Elizabeth, most of us had visibly relaxed. She was certainly no disciplinarian and liked to digress at enormous length away from the topics we were nominally studying, telling elaborate tales from her working life or personal past.

Elizabeth had not worked for the Underground for long, but had many years service with British Rail in various capacities. Bringing us up to date she said she was now living happily with a boyfriend, but had twice been married. Her first husband had died young from a brain tumour. Her second husband had taken to beating her and she walked out on him. She seemed to have a large number of children, at least one of whom was mentally sub-normal and another, grown child, was gay. Her mother was an unashamed racist, for ever rhetorically asking when *they* would leave England and go back where *they came from.*

I sensed it was almost as if, with each improbable admission, Elizabeth was raising the stakes, daring us not to study or to attend to her instruction squeezed in between details of her sad fate. As if she were saying, 'You owe me a few days of effort; just look at me, always grasping on to the shitty end of the stick, but have I stopped smiling, even for a minute?' Yes, everyone liked Elizabeth, but I began to suspect she was highly expert at manipulating groups of strangers. She was successfully playing on our collective sympathies and I wondered what she would do next. Arrive in a wheelchair?

Announce her own, terminal, illness? Kneel down and plead with us directly? Soft skills were at work all right, it was like being slowly smothered with a silken cushion. You die smiling and thinking how nice it feels.

(26)

We had just spent the morning discussing problem-solving in general, learning to differentiate between genuine questions which can be answered informatively and complaints disguised as questions which don't seek answers, but are only framed to reduce the questioner's feelings of anger or frustration. Elizabeth explained that complaints were mostly emotional outpourings, where customers were not interested in a careful discussion based on agreed information and would resent any attempts to establish a scientific or Socratic approach: 'Ah, Phaedrus, must we not first agree on exactly what we understand by the words *late running*?'

(27)

It was lunchtime and I went to the canteen wondering what an EGO-Gram would look like. We had been introduced to a psychological system called Transactional Analysis, where the EGO-Gram was a central concept.

I accepted the need to 'Know Thyself' and always welcomed the possibility of a new means to achieve this. Balanced against this was an inner voice which warned me that most personality assessment systems were crude admixtures of flattery and randomly generalised criticisms. It had always struck me as significant how susceptible we all are to nonsense: for example, that most of us keenly study our horoscopes, often reading them aloud to friends. We are suggestible and seem to lack internally generated self-confidence to such an extent that enormous amounts of time, energy and attention are each day devoted to major self-affirmation activity.

(28)

To draw up an EGO-Gram you simply had to answer sixty questions. They were loaded with value judgements and the answers were classified as adult, parental or childish responses, and projected Venn-diagram fashion; the chart was a visual representation of our progress towards human maturity.

Something about this type of test forces me to adopt a persona not my own. I feel compelled to assume an imaginary personality and answer away in character – and I am sure this is a fairly common English habit and is one reason why market surveys always seem to be wrong. The questioner may make adjustments of a per-centage point or two – a so-called margin of error – but should instead wonder whether cultural factors mean that all the answers are 'errors'. This reminded me of early maps marked with sites which mean 'Go away!' or 'Leave me alone!' or 'I don't know!' in the local lan-guages, given in response to the unwelcome question, 'Where am I?' By questioning me, while you are a com-plete stranger, you invite me to lie, because my real sentiments are NONE OF YOUR BUSINESS!

(29)

Until you can establish a basis for sincere interaction, it is always necessary to question the classification of what is actually taking place.

(30)

The EGO-Gram statements included: *Long hair seems to have to compensate for small brains nowadays.* Did my baldness mean I had a huge brain?! *Being humble makes me feel good;* and *I love swapping stories about the 'old days'.* What would Dan and Dexter make of this? They didn't look the type to swap nostalgic reminiscences about their infancies.

As I read the EGO-Gram questions I thought about Douglas Adams's *The Hitchhiker's Guide to the Galaxy.* A huge computer, Deep Thought, is programmed to answer the question 'What is the meaning of Life, the Universe and Everything?' and, after seven and a half million years of processing, answers 42.

(31)

We are addicted to asking questions without attending to whether or not we can make use (or sense) of the answers.

(32)

Totting up the numbers, I found I had achieved a satisfyingly large number of adult responses. I knew this was flattery but part of me still responded – yes, yes, confirmation of my maturity by scientific methods at long last. I was also more nurturing parent than critical parent, which seemed wrong. And more adapted child than natural child, which I didn't feel able to evaluate as I was unable to find out what an adapted child might be.

We went round the class. What embarrassing secrets would Transactional Analysis reveal? The short answer is most EGO-Grams seemed to resemble each other. What is the difference between a 5 Critical Parent/3 Nurturing Parent/15 Adult/ 4 Adapted Child/ 2 Natural Child person on the one hand and a 3 Critical Parent/ 5 Nurturing Parent/ 15 Adult/ 2 Adapted Child/ 4 Natural Child person on the other? I still had no idea when Elizabeth explained that all the answers were fine and indicated we were all great, amazing, well balanced and that this just confirmed all her earlier remarks about how brilliant we all were! 'Wow!' she said, as if the evidence of our collective excellence had just piled up so thick and fast it was too much for her to take in.

Was this just a parlour game used by lecturers to involve the class? Like asking someone to assume a French identity, say, Jean-Paul, handing him a *ballon* and telling him to *jouez avec* it, prior to predictably asking what he is doing? Jean-Paul, *qu'est-ce que vous faites?*

(33)

When people are upset or angry, Customer Care instructed us to try to behave in such a way as to switch the enraged back into the Land of Reason, somewhat hopefully labelled 'adult' in this schema. Apparently there were several ways to do this, such as by asking factual questions, phrased so as to elicit information in the response, denying the emotionally satisfying but non-adult sulky yes-or-no monosyllabic reply. This trick had to be balanced against firing off questions at customers who were not yet close to the adult boundary we sought to haul them over. They must first be soothed, like the naughty children they were.

(34)

Dealing with Complaints led on to Assault Awareness. Judith and Shaz sat next to me in the canteen, still buzzing with the implications of what we were being taught. 'I'm taking no shit from anyone, man,' said Judith scowling. 'I'll tell the first one to dis me where to get off. They don't pay me to take crap . . .' She was interrupted by her mobile phone and had to go outside to improve the signal reception.

Shaz, who'd been nodding agreement, was muttering the phrase 'combat-ready mind' over and over, and looked up from his fish and chips to say he liked that; he had a combat-ready mind and was really looking forward to going over the top and slapping the arseholes down.

Had everyone gone mad?

(35)

Assault Awareness involved some strange advice. Rule 1: *Always look a customer in the eye.* Rule 2: *Keep a safe distance.* Rule 3: *Don't react to verbal abuse.* Rule 4: *Call for assistance or if no assistance is available retreat to the wooden sentry box.* I had yet to learn about the Station Assistant who, having locked himself inside a wooden sentry box, was picked up and thrown on to the tracks.

Bravado apart, we all wondered how rough it really was out there. The job didn't have the profile of, say, door security at a night club, but I remembered occasionally seeing news items in the *Evening Standard* about a rise in knife assaults against Tube employees. But did this mean an increase from a single to two incidents – or something out of Kurosawa's *Seven Samurai*?

(36)

After lunch Elizabeth said we could leave early, but before heading home we must first go to the Clothing Department in Acton to collect our uniforms. Everyone seemed cheered by the prospect of an early escape.

Standing in a long queue outside a Portakabin. The head of the queue dissolves inside the building in stops and starts and after an hour of shuffling it is our turn. The shipyard-like scenery and the desultory queueing make me think of East Germany or Poland under communism. Judith loudly proclaims that we would have gone home half an hour ago if it had been a normal day, if we hadn't been allowed to leave 'early'. Like an Eastern European I ignore this 'bad news' and calmly wait and watch.

(37)

I am measured and questioned about sizes and then one man ticks off items on a list as another runs around the large room selecting stuff and bringing it back to pile next to where I am standing. This is done very quickly and I am asked to try on only one or two things: the shoes, the hat. The only cap which fits is enormous. It is designed to be worn by someone at least a foot taller and resembles the outsized headgear favoured by the most senior Soviet generals. I think of a helicopter landing pad, but know feeling ridiculous is a sensation that fades quite quickly.

The pile is transferred into bags and parcels: there are six shirts, four pairs of trousers, two jackets, two overcoats, two pairs of Doctor Martens shoes, a belt, two clip-on ties, a hi-visibility vest, a plastic keyring, two jumpers and the huge cap, complete with cap band and badge. The trendy Tube boxer shorts with the slogan 'Mind the Gap' printed next to the fly, I was disappointed to learn, are reserved for the general public and do not form part of our uniform.

I stumble outside with the huge number of bags. This is the most 'shopping' I have ever tried to carry at one time. I think of taking a cab, but quickly decide to go home by Underground instead. Struggling is good for me, isn't it? And the journey is free, after all.

(38)

In marketing the word 'free' means the cost is concealed. Nothing is ever free. There is always a price to pay, in terms of money, or effort, or time, or quality.

(39)

During the recruitment interviews I had been asked at least a dozen times if I had a problem wearing a uniform and had answered, quite falsely, none at all. The point of uniforms is to make everything outwardly the same and, if possible, by a knock-on psychological effect inwardly the same too. This was something I rejected conceptually, but knew that content mattered much more than the container and so as long as you can resist any culture of conformity which went along with the uniform you would be OK.

(40)

Modern western culture is built around externals, around appearances. Something must first resemble what we expect it to look like before we take notice. We readily accept authoritative statements made by our culture's authority figures (our witch doctors) – experts, pundits, commentators, scientists, men in white coats. We are conditioned a thousand times each day by ornament and display, by drama and excitement. Look! It's flashing and making a strange noise – it must be about to do something really special!

You are standing next to a saint at a bus stop, but having no perceptive abilities see only the housewife, office worker, man in overalls. Inner nature is completely concealed by concentration on outwardness. Attracted to a beautiful face, you fail to notice the heart of stone and capacity for betrayal . . .

How many times must this happen before realising

that mistaking the container for the content is the cause of much misery?

(41)

While teaching children in Japan, whenever I took a straw poll, youngsters always voted in favour of maintaining uniforms at school, saying they liked them and would otherwise stand out in unwelcome ways. This contrasts strongly with English kids of the same age who abandon their uniforms in a flash if ever allowed to do so or when unsupervised. Yet the obvious conclusion, that this somehow indicates that English culture promotes individuality when compared with that of Japan, is far from the truth. It simply means that there is a ranking scheme where uniforms mean different things in different places and that these are connected with perceptions of status.

Schoolboy or student in English society is a low-status occupation implying subordination. But this isn't so in Japan, where it's thought normal for children. And what of other 'uniforms', such as denims, or all black clothes, or designer training shoes. They convey something more important to the wearer than 'sameness', the real message of a uniform. They are, of course, badges of tribal identity.

(42)

Bombay, Sahar International, just landed to attend a friend's wedding. Standing in line prior to some form of official questioning always makes me very nervous. In all such interactions I feel I have something to hide – such as the opinion that I dislike officials – and must consciously master myself. I know someone who was strip-searched and detained for six hours on entering America, so-called Land of the Free, for accidentally ticking yes to the question about intending to commit an act of terrorism while visiting, misreading 'terrorism' as 'tourism'. I knew it paid to be invisible, but had such places been equipped with sophisticated devices calibrated to monitor the vital signs of those queueing, mine would have confirmed me as a hardened fugitive, perhaps someone who had just escaped from prison and was now 'on the run'. I could hardly wait to flee into the craziness of the Bombay night.

We stopped at a red light and a beggar without hands tapped his wrist stumps against the window, appealing for help. I had no coins, had yet to change any money, but for a second wondered how he would take a contribution towards financing his miserable existence were I to lower the window to give him something; would he stick out his tongue like a communicant, casting me as a sort of priest and a coin as the host, or would he use his stumps like chopsticks? We left him, the driver unaware of my strange thoughts, and speeding along again the idea was quickly sloughed off and left behind by the side of the road.

(43)

The end of the year and the beginning of another in India, like everywhere else, is a time for celebration. Indian fireworks are quite unique, however, and bear a close resemblance to munitions. Safety considerations are ignored. Rockets fired horizontally, often launched by hand, hiss past inches from your face.

Walking towards the Bombay Yacht Club where we had agreed to meet friends, I bought some sparklers from a street seller, only they were much larger than normal and the combustible material was an alarming shade of scarlet. As we turned the corner to approach the club a beggar without legs sped towards us on a crude skateboard, using small blocks of wood in his hands to propel himself. He shot across the ground and immediately began importuning for a small coin, for some acknowledgement that having no legs in one of the poorest cities in the world deserved whatever help may be available.

We could run a tab in the Yacht Club and no one had any money. An inspiration made me light one of the sparklers and hand it over. It fizzed alarmingly and made a noise like a bomb about to go off. As we walked away I turned and looked back. The crippled street beggar was spinning around and around on his skateboard, laughing madly and tracing infinity signs in phosphorescent white light against the black of the last night of the year.

(44)

The Customer Care Quiz, by way of introduction, unhelpfully said: 'This self-study quiz will enable you to: * Identify who your customer are (sic) . . .' It was a multi-choice test and we had thirty minutes to answer twenty-six questions. Question 11 asked:

People are made up of:

54%   67.4%   70%   72.8% water

We all knew the correct answer was 72.8 per cent, as this improbable statistic had been drummed into us by rote. Later I did some research to confirm the oddly precise percentage and discovered that its precision was a sleight of hand. It was more accurate to say the human body is between 50 and 65 per cent water, and that this varies between the genders, with men having more water in their bodies than women. Moreover, not all body parts have the same water content: blood is, unsurprisingly, 90 per cent water; bone 30 per cent; brain 75 per cent and muscle 72 per cent. Fat is only 15 per cent water and as women generally have higher body fat this explains their overall lower water content.

Straining dimly I wondered why we had been taught this counter-intuitive information. Was it because we seem to be solid rather than three-quarters 'liquid' and this was a way of emphasising our insubstantiality? Was it the lesson of water flowing, forming itself to any existing shape? That it was crucial to maintain life itself? How this related to the business of caring for customers was never made clear.

(45)

A drop of rain dripping from the clouds
Felt ashamed when it saw the vastness of the sea.
'Where there is a sea, what am I?
If it is there, then I am nowhere.'
When it saw itself with humility

An oyster adopted it and nourished it with heart;
Fate carried on its work to such an extent
That it became a celebrated pearl, befitting a King
It attained sublimeness when it humbled itself;
Knocking at the door of non-existence, it became existent.

BOSTAN-I-SAADI (Trans MIRZA AQIL-HUSSAIN, BARLAS)

(46)

I completed the test and read the final message which appeared below question 26. It took the form of an expression of goodwill:

> Thank you for completing this test. Training Services/Soft Skills unit would like to wish you well for the rest of your training here at Ashfield House and the very best of luck in your new job as a London Underground Station Assistant. We remind you to be proud of your job, and yourself, and always think:
>
> **Customer,\ People (you), Business**

I had no idea what this could possibly mean.

(47)

Elizabeth told me she had really enjoyed teaching us and wanted to stay in touch. She wrote her home telephone number on a piece of paper torn from an exercise book and handed it over. I put it in my wallet. Something about the sad voice she used to invite me to call her whenever I might be free for a drink suggested she doubted I would ever do so.

(48)

Saturday began no differently from a weekday as I climbed into my still-unfamiliar uniform, leaving the flat early enough to arrive in Acton for the 9 a.m. class start. I took a seat at the back of the classroom, next to the window. I did this without thinking and not because I hoped to gaze out into freedom, at the warm summer sunshine.

Something in the atmosphere warned me that the corporate culture of Acton differed from that of West Kensington. There were more men with dirty hands and oily faces walking around – it was an engineering depot – and in other ways it seemed a more masculine place, like a mine or a shipyard. Hardly anyone was smiling and everyone seemed to smoke. Ashfield House was simply an office block, equally divided between the sexes, multi-cultural and diverse in comparison.

(49)

Frank came in, wrote his name on the board and took the register. Everyone was there, except Shaz and Dan. Even Dexter had arrived and was quietly dozing in a corner.

Frank would teach us Fire Safety and Awareness and he handed out an A4 booklet, bound appropriately in scarlet card and illustrated with two line-drawings of fire extinguishers. He started to explain what we would be doing and what he would be covering. About a minute into Frank's introductory remarks about the three things we need to start a fire, Dan walked in.

Like me and one or two others Dan was wearing his

uniform, although it was optional at this stage in our training. Frank testily asked him why he was late and he mumbled something I couldn't catch and then said he was very sorry twice in a louder but humble voice, looking down and shuffling. God, I thought, ten years old again, what must we do to get this job? Frank told him to sit down at once and began again at a faster pace, as if to catch up like a tape deck on the dub setting, and in an irritated tone.

'What three things do we need for a fire?' he asked again. Had I not already glanced at the notes I would have confidently answered matches, a lighter and, remembering Piggy's spectacles from Golding's *Lord of the Flies*, a magnifying glass; but I knew the correct answer to be HEAT, OXYGEN and FUEL. Everyone parroted this answer in unison. By now we had all learned to cheat, as if rehearsing for a North Korean State occasion and Frank's face twitched as if we had beaten him to the punchline in a favourite joke he was telling. You could see he was assessing whether we were mocking him, but didn't know for sure. Some kind of struggle seemed to be taking place behind his eyes.

The classroom door opened and in walked Shaz smiling the smile of someone who had yet to meet Frank, someone whose mind was still set at 'Elizabeth' on the teacher spectrum, expecting mild reasonableness. He was also wearing his uniform, but had left off the clip-on tie – a joke accessory, like a clown's red nose – and had his shirt open at the neck. He looked smart, even dashing. His smiling face was that of a young man free of the cares a few more years of adult life would bring, and enjoying summer. Before he could utter a word or begin to explain his tardy appearance Frank had thrown down his notes and, seizing Shaz's sleeve, bustled him towards the door. The look on Frank's face was instantly apoplectic, menacing, and seemed to promise imminent violence.

Was he taking Shaz outside for a kicking? Should we rescue our classmate from the teacher who had clearly gone mad? Or more accurately arrived mad, for we hadn't yet had time to light the blue touch paper and watch him explode. It was him not us. Or would Shaz, like the trained martial artist he was, react without thought to such hostility, leaping in the air to spin around a couple of times and smash his uniformed knee into Frank's foaming chops? I wanted to jump up and run across the classroom to look through the glass in the door, but something kept me in my chair, straining to hear the sound of muffled screaming.

Part of me hoped there would be a fight. We would all get to go home early if our teacher had to be taken to accident and emergency. But a more sensible part didn't want Shaz sacrificing his chance of a good summer job simply to buy us a reprieve on a few hours of boredom. Perhaps not quite understanding why he was the focus of such sudden vehemence, he did nothing except switch off his smile, allowing himself to be propelled through the door into the corridor and beyond and then all the way home; and by the effects of momentum to be forced to change out of his uniform and then to play cricket for the remainder of the lovely warm morning far away from the airless classrooms of Acton Town. Shaz had been shown the red card; sent home for being ten minutes late.

It certainly didn't take much to inflame Frank, perhaps causing him to fail us. These teachers must know they held us in their power and could stand between us and the jobs we were all trying to obtain.

Of course, apart from insanity there was another reason explaining why Frank had behaved in this way. It was a classic heckler-killing strategy exploited by many experienced teachers: show new students who is boss at the very beginning and everything will then go smoothly. You retain complete control. But weren't such draconian methods suited only to teaching unruly children, not to lecturing adults, some of whom were mature, had tasted life's bitter moments, could be counted on, reasoned with, surely?

(50)

What is a teacher? A teacher is someone who has what you need and knows how to give it to you.

(51)

But Frank was here to talk about fire, not pedagogy. There would be no debate and he slid seemlessly into a discussion of terms I had given no thought to since O-level physics over twenty years before: convection, conduction, radiation. The warm, airless, classroom was subversive. Who really cared? They all just meant fire.

(52)

My experiences with fire to date were nothing to feel confident about. At twelve I had tried to extinguish a flaming frying pan with a soda siphon. This caused a fireball which destroyed my mother's favourite Laura

Ashley kitchen curtains and a hideous corn dolly of significant sentimental worth permanently stationed next to the stove and which had been retrieved unscathed from a family home hit by a V2 rocket during the Second World War. Ten years later, helping a friend burn the pollarded branches of the vast rows of pruned fruit trees on his huge estate, I encouraged a damp bonfire with a can of petrol retrieved from an outbuilding. No one was nearby to witness the minor explosion it caused, blasting me over a hedge and singeing my eyebrows so badly they took five weeks to regrow.

Most recently, in Japan, I had been quietly smoking my pipe in the early hours of the morning in one of the two six-tatami-mat rooms which comprised the apartment I shared with two friends. The sliding door to the next room opened and one sleepy friend, blinking at the light cast from my room, moaned about my pipe. As the door was slid back a little further it revealed that the thick cloud of smoke troubling him was not coming from my pipe but from the room he was sleeping in. My futon, rolled out and waiting for me, was on fire, ignited by a reading light placed face down by the second friend, still sound asleep, to 'get the light out of his face'. We had carefully to extinguish the futon, hacking off the burning part with a kitchen cleaver and throwing it into the bath, and then to disperse the smoke. All this without alerting our neighbours who would have forced us to move, justifiably fearing fire above all else, when living in a wooden house, divided by paper walls and heated with ancient kerosene burners.

(53)

A friend who had signed up for a four-day woodcraft course excitedly explained how he had learned to make fire using a bow drill. He had made the drill too – and then had produced fire from nowhere. He told me it was like magic and, as it involved a knack, provided deep satisfaction. He showed me a rope he had plaited from the fibres of a common plant and a small fish hook made from strips of bark and a thorn, which looked like something from the Ancient Britons section of a museum. I could understand his enthusiasm. Acquiring skills is a form of initiation into a mystery. It is really something to be able to make fire.

(54)

Instead of the practical fire-fighting skills and knowledge I had hoped for, or even a few distilled rules of thumb gleaned from the King's Cross fire of 1987 in which thirty-one people died in under sixteen minutes, we watched a video of the Bradford Stadium fire and then, like interior decorators, examined the colour scheme of a range of fire extinguishers. This was followed by a short quiz to see which fire safety slogans we could remember. When we took a mid-morning break Frank was first out of the door, moving quite suddenly like a rocket shot out of a milk bottle.

The fire extinguishers were red, black, cream, green; they contained different materials and were designed for fighting different types of fire. We rote learned which was which and I presumed we would soon get to extinguish one or two controlled fires ignited in some suitable receptacle, such as a fireproof bin, to learn how to use them. But there was to be no hands-on training. Should we actually have to fight a fire we would have to learn at that time.

(55)

After we had reviewed silencing and responding to alarms, it was time to talk about suspect packages, which, of course, meant bombs. Elizabeth had told me that London Underground had a private arrangement with the IRA; that the Provos had offered a stand-still agreement not to plant bombs on the Tube network. I wondered at her source of information and also whether the IRA got something in return? Free travel? Discounts at the Transport Museum shop in Covent Garden?

(56)

The only fact which went beyond common sense in our bomb class was that we should immediately switch off our radios in the vicinity of anything we thought might be a bomb for fear of detonating it ourselves with radio signals.

Beyond this solitary useful fact we were comprehensively briefed on bomb dangers by means of a slogan:

Beware
Observe everything
Maybe it's nothing
But don't take a chance

Still inform the following –
* Line Controller
* British Transport Police (Auto 999)
* Station Supervisor

Remember: Bombs can come in all SHAPES and sizes

I noticed how the first letters of the catchy slogans, read top to bottom (vertical thinking?) spelt BOMBS and was lost in admiration for the author of these notes. It was really helpful to be able to remember the words Beware and Observe, although Maybe, But and Still were, I thought, of less real value.

We were tested once more, this time on bombs, and having passed were each issued with a Fire Safety Certificate. I took mine home and put it in a file. No one ever asked to see it or referred to it ever again.

(57)

Shaz arrived just as class was beginning and the first opportunity to question him was during the morning coffee and comfort break. I knew how much the newly adult resent being treated as children and expected a bitter tirade against fiery Frank. But Shaz seemed to have forgotten what happened two days before.

'So what happened on the other side of the door?' I said. 'What door?' said Shaz. 'Saturday morning. You attended the fire safety class for about ten seconds, never to reappear. What did Frank say to you?' 'He was Frank, huh? Well, he was certainly frank with me, just told me to go home. Said he was sick of repeating himself and I would have to come back the following week. No big deal, I got to play some cricket. What did you do?' he asked. 'We watched a video and tried to remember what's inside a fire extinguisher by its colour. And we did bombs,' I replied. 'Bombs? Cool, like defusing and stuff?' said Shaz. 'No, more like assuming anything you can't open is a bomb and calling out the cavalry even when you know it is just someone's forgotten luggage. And that you are supposed to put out burning customers with a fire blanket, not a CO_2 extinguisher.'

(58)

Following the afternoon coffee break, Barbara, tasked with lecturing us on signalling and track safety theory, appeared holding a length of metal, an object which resembled in size and design a device for immobilising a car. 'This is a SCD,' said Barbara, holding the thing up and waving it in an arc like a magic wand. She seemed to expect that we might already know what a SCD was, what it was for, or come to understand it just by looking at it. 'What's a SCD?' asked Dan, speaking for us all. 'It's a short circuiting device,' answered Barbara. 'It's used to safely isolate traction current. You place one at the front and another at the rear of a train so the track is dead.'

(59)

A short circuit occurs when a route offers a smaller resistance to an electrical charge than the 'normal' circuit. Electricity takes the path of least resistance.

In human affairs we can classify many habits and obsessive compulsive behaviour or addictions as short circuits. They arise from the need for immediate mood gratification and quickly become traps. People so afflicted behave as if controlled from outside themselves. That a short circuit is operating is necessary knowledge in the process of repair.

(60)

There were only two things to remember. Secure one end of the SCD against one of the traction current rails first, then, looking away to avoid being blinded by arching sparks, sharply lower the other end of the SCD against the other rail, letting go at the same time. It also paid to position your feet so that you didn't form part of the circuit you were hoping to short. It didn't seem too hard – but I had forgotten how many find a practical task involving doing two things at once quite a challenge.

Barbara, who had shorted more circuits than anyone could remember, demonstrated twice and told us we had to have a go in turn. Dan stared at the rails as he lowered the SCD with a resounding clang and was, he learned later, now blind. Judith also surrendered her sight. Dexter, blind too according to Barbara, had his eyes shut as he lowered the device, but Barbara didn't notice. I had watched her closely and set about performing the movements exactly as demonstrated, exaggeratedly looking off into the middle distance at the nearby and very ugly office buildings as if my life depended on it. Barbara seemed pleased that someone in our group had managed to retain their sight. I wondered why we were practising on a piece of dummy rail on a grass verge outside an office building, rather than real track with live current. There had to come a time when simulation must give way to the real thing. *Was reality to form no part of our training?*

(61)

Learning by doing may involve risk-taking, which may be eliminated or reduced by simulating the activity in a form where these elements are removed. However, unless the trainee is not aware of the simulation, believes the situation to be real, the knowledge that risk has been reduced or removed will have a disabling effect. The very reactions which are hardest to train – such as the mastery of fear, for example – may not occur at all. Only through effective dissimulation may a simulated experience serve the function of a real one.

(62)

I had forgotten the trackwalk. We had been nervously anticipating this outing since we found out about it on the first day, but no one had mentioned when or if this would take place and so we had forgotten about it.

Once again we gathered in Frank's classroom in Acton. The day before we had been told to wear only certain types of shoes. The trackwalk was to follow the Piccadilly Line between Northfields and South Ealing stations. It was only a short distance, but we had to cross the track by stepping over live rails. Dodging trains didn't concern me; they were big and noisy and could be seen and heard from a considerable distance. *Electricity is invisible and is known only by its effects.* We had discussed if

the charge was enough to kill you and the consensus
was that you needed to fall across both live rails to risk
death by electrocution.

Standing in a single file, everyone in bright orange
vests. Frank and two others who were to act as protection masters sported armbands and carried lamps and
flags. The atmosphere of a school outing had dried up
and everyone seemed visibly to concentrate as we set
off. The gravel crunched beneath my feet and I tried to
simultaneously look ahead and behind. We were drawn
up in a tight group and I didn't want to be jostled off
balance.

A blackbird perched in a hawthorn by the side of
the track sounded an alarm call. A whistle answered
immediately after, as if echoing the bird. A train was
approaching and we all stood carefully to one side as
the Heathrow-bound Piccadilly Line Tube passed packed
with tourists and businessmen bound for who knows
where. We too were on a journey, were following someone, like the driver of the Piccadilly train, who had travelled this way many times and knew just what to do
and where to tread. We crossed the track without incident and, feeling suddenly unburdened, crunched our
way on to the platform at South Ealing as another train,
this time almost empty, hurtled past in the opposite
direction.

Everyone stood around grinning. We'd done it. The
trackwalk was over and we were still alive, still in one
piece. There had been no spontaneous amputations by
the wheels of passing locomotives and no electrocutions.
I suppose we knew it wasn't much really, just a wander
down a few hundred yards of dirt, a hop over some
rails, and standing aside while a large, noisy train rattles
past, safely out of reach; but we'd so talked up the

hazardous nature of this part of our training, it felt cathartic.

Like a shaman, Frank materialised a symbol of our success, a badge of each individual triumph. Reaching inside his jacket he extracted a bundle of folded pieces of paper, each one held inside a clear plastic wallet. He looked at them, sorted them into name order and then began handing them out. They were our official licences. As I took mine I realised I was now fully trained. It was time to go to work.

PART II

Tunnel Visions

tunnel – . . . 3. a prolonged period of
difficulty or suffering . . .

CONCISE OXFORD DICTIONARY (9TH EDITION)

Where there is no vision, the people perish

PROVERBS XXIX, 18

(1)

Nothing happens until something moves. Life resides in motion. My life had definitely slowed and the distances travelled diminished nearly to nothing. Walking along the middle circulating area – Oxford Circus Station is arranged like a triple-decker sandwich – I crept towards escalators 9 and 10, pacing out the corridor in the steady lope I had recently adopted. Omar, another SA, gracile and of Sudanese descent, moved so effortlessly and with such noble insouciance, it was easy to imagine him crossing not Platform 5 but huge expanses of sub-Saharan scrub leading a camel. Only Salman Qureshi, a hyperactive Supervisor who kept going all day at a terrible pace through sheer momentum, always moved about at breakneck speeds – like a light brown version of Alice's white rabbit, holding a clipboard instead of a pocket-watch, one minute there, the next gone, already engaged on the next task.

(2)

Slow pacing achieved several things at once: it was calming and also exuded a measure of authority and knowledge – I pace in this way as I am familiar with this place and do not need to shuffle about in a panic. It was necessary to walk this way to relax and by relaxing to resist the ever-present urge to punish rude customers. Pacing kept me level and each day I walked miles, every one on unforgiving concrete slabs and moving metal.

(3)

I step off the escalators, automatically scanning the two fire extinguishers hanging on their brackets for signs of having been moved since I last looked at them, yesterday morning. No one had touched them, the mark in the dust traced from extinguisher to the wall was still lined up precisely. Walking towards the end of the passageway which connected Platform 6 (my home) to Platform 4, I turn left on to the platform and turn again, this time to the right, to begin my arriving on the platform rituals.

These were safety checks and I always did them in exactly the same order. First, wander down to the Headwall – the front-of-the-train end of the platform – to check the seal of the Headwall Tunnel Telephone is intact. Check locked doors along the platform are, in fact, locked. Check the public phone works and that it accepts coins as well as credit and prepaid phone cards, as it is the only coin phone in the station within the barriers. Check the strip lights are not flickering or dead. No obvious build-up of inflammable materials on the rails. Fire extinguishers and hoses intact and in date. First-aid stretcher un-nibbled by the station mice, and still in its purpose-built wall-mounted cupboard, where there is room for me to store abandoned newspapers to pick up later, before ascending into the overground world where newspaper reading is allowed. Check the Autophone, the Underground's dedicated internal telephone network. And finally, the public address system, where the first announcement of the day will reveal its condition: a spectrum ranging from poor to nonfunctional.

(4)

Walking and moving slowly meant it took more time than strictly necessary to conclude these checks, but there was no particular hurry. Safety checks had a purpose that made sense and despite their repetitive nature and the mechanising effects of doing the same things in the same order each weekday, I preferred these routines to work which had far less obvious utility: such as asking customers to stand clear of the closing doors. Did anyone actually take notice of this formulaic warning? No one ever came up to me to thank me for warning of the impending danger of sudden door closure. Thousands of warnings, all unheeded. Cassandra with an extension mike and a lack of conviction in the voice.

(5)

Speed, which becomes a virtue when it is found in a horse, by itself has no advantages.

MOHAMMED EL GHAZALI

There's a joke about someone painting a door. Painting in a panic, slapping on the paint just as fast as is humanly possible. 'Why are you painting so fast?' asks an onlooker. 'Well,' replies the painter, 'just look in this pot. There's only a little paint left . . . and I really want to finish the door before it runs out.' The way we all scurry about often calls this to mind. The explanation for our hyperactivity and hurry seems to be, 'I have to move this fast to improve the quality of my life.' But this in turn begs further questions: when will you stop improving and start living? Isn't this minute of life as good and as real as the next one?

(6)

I had done my fair share of dashing about, having lived most of my life in the chaos of huge cities. In Tokyo I met someone who had developed a strange and chronic pain in his left wrist, which he eventually realised was caused by constantly looking at his watch. In London it would be foolish to try to plan precisely how long it would take to go from A to B. In Tokyo all you need is a timetable of the local train and subway systems and an accurate watch. If your watch stops, you can reset it by the time of the next train to arrive. In London things do not work quite like that.

(7)

Only thoughts which come from walking have any value.
NIETZSCHE

As the first horde of the morning flowed out of a train, moving around my stationary form, like a river around a rock, I reflected on body language. Not the stuff featured in documentaries, which always seem to concentrate on how lovers synchronise their movements when drinking together in a bar, or how repeatedly looking away to the right suggests you are lying. But something more fundamental: how we move. I began to develop a system for classifying walks, not silly walks, although there were plenty of those to choose from, but the small range of common or garden walks, and at the same time to consider what, if anything, they told me about the walkers.

Young men and teenagers wearing training shoes often ambled along using what Tom Wolfe once called the Pimp Roll. Feet everted, hips opened out and pushed forward, shoulders bobbing in time, a lot of arm swing. This walk was designed as a warning: I'm bad, so beware! But if you kept watching, the clues to the real underlying character were there too. Perhaps birdlike movements of the head to see if anyone was watching, revealing that this particular Bad Boy is shy.

The Pimp Roll was cousin to a walk used by construction workers and anyone who put in a lot of time with weights in a gym. Again the feet were turned out and the heels used to pull the body forward from the hips. And the groin was thrust forward – was this a primate thing, alpha males leading with their genitals? – and there was a lot of upper body swagger as a sort of counterpoint to the rotating hips. Unlike the Pimp Roll there was no direct challenge in this walk and sometimes it seemed as if there was a good-natured humour underlying the movements, perhaps born of physical confidence. It was a body walk first and foremost: I am a body man, I use my body to earn my living. *I am my body*.

The Forward Fall was a walk used by the more cerebral. It involved losing your balance and falling forward and just managing to slide a foot in before toppling over – and this is then repeated with the other leg. It was a walk I felt fairly sure the walker would be very surprised to see if it was filmed and shown to them. It involved to a remarkable degree a lack of self-awareness. Was the walker perhaps always lost inside himself, only very lightly connecting to the physical world around him?

The very tall often employed the Knee Flick. The hip flexor muscles are ignored in this walk and the lower part of the leg is flicked into place using the muscles of the knee. The upper body is held very still and the impression is of a wading bird, a heron or stork. This walk seemed to say something like 'my legs are so long, they demand all the action'.

(8)

Shoes, it seemed to me, get in the way. They come between you and a consciousness of what you are doing many times a minute with your feet. It then becomes a fairly simple thing to walk in a way which is neither natural nor beneficial.

And in the case of women's shoes they may even kill you! The British Standards Institute, I had just learned, was pressing for women's platform shoes to carry a safety warning following 'an epidemic of killer shoes'. This was not much of an exaggeration. A twenty-five-year-old Japanese nursery school worker had recently fallen off her platform sandals, hit her head and died – and there were many more cases of broken bones and twisted joints. Literally, fashion to die for.

(9)

There has been no time in recorded history in which man has not decorated himself and his environment to enhance and achieve pleasing effects. Self-ornamentation has, however, long outstripped a finely developed aesthetic sensibility and can now clearly be identified as driven by the consumer society. Ornaments of a bewildering variety have become for many of us a necessity, their absence unimaginable. It seems unlikely to change, until there is no longer a profit for the ornament-makers.

Compulsive self-ornamentation relies on being able to induce a deep fear of inadequacy in the initially ornament-frcc, in those in the pre-ornamental state. Only a freak or a fool will choose not to take advantage of our wares! Look at what everyone else is doing if you want to know the right way to behave!

(10)

A security alert at Piccadilly Circus had just halted the Bakerloo Line between Charing Cross and Paddington in both directions. I strolled across to help Mr Ojo, who was looking after Platform 4, the northbound Bakerloo Line and the platform parallel to my own private world on Platform 6.

Platform 4 and Platform 6 were strangely dissimilar. There was something distinctly classier about 6; both in terms of its wholesome appearance, cleaner, lighter and benefiting from the attractive contrast of the Victoria Line's white and cornflower blue livery. It was the same blue you see everywhere in the residential district of Sidi Bou Said in Tunis, where the intensity of the light seems to demand the soft, cool blue. You could rest your eyes on that blue and call to mind water, the source of all life.

Bakerloo brown was, by contrast, uninspiring. We were always finding dog turds in the passageways leading to the Bakerloo Line. Sometimes these offerings were missed for a day or so and were transformed into coprolite by the dry wind emitting from the tunnels.

I began at once to explain what was going on to the knot of passengers who immediately clustered round me. I soothed, using a submissive, lowered tone of voice – I had learned how you spoke was far more important than the actual information content of what you said. The trouble with a security alert is that it is impossible to predict how long any delay will last, which is precisely what everyone wants to know. It usually turns out to be a false alarm: a forgotten bag containing nothing but a packed lunch and a few files. Once we unzipped an abandoned bright red holder, ignoring the regulations and risking vaporisation should it turn out to be a booby-trapped bomb. Inside the otherwise empty bag were two small rubber crocodiles.

I tried to help everyone, suggesting alternative routes for those hurrying to catch trains at Marylebone and Paddington, while advising the less time-pressed to remain on the platform as I expected it would 'clear down' in only a few minutes. Behind me a woman's voice demanded immediate attention. The voice was strident and shrill, sharp-edged and thrusting like a dagger in the back. I turned to answer her, fixing my smile, and was confronted by a portly blind lady holding the lead and harness of a Golden Labrador guide dog.

'I'm already an hour late,' she whinged. 'It's all because of the inefficiency of your staff at Mile End.' There had also been a hold-up on the Central Line. These things hardly ever happened one at a time, and sometimes we faced meltdown. Security alerts were particularly 'infectious', as staff throughout the system copied each other's degree of nervousness, in case it turned out to be *the real thing*. 'I'm sorry,' I said. 'What may I do for you?' She continued to rant and, as she rejected each apology and suggestion offered, the tone of my voice began to change, allowing a note of frustration to creep into my soft delivery. 'What would you like me to do?' I asked again flatly. 'Would you like to leave the station and continue by surface transport?' She looked crosser still. 'I don't want to inconvenience other passengers. I've had arguments here before about stopping escalators,' she moaned.

All at once I saw she was a shrew, permanently cross, inconsolable. It didn't make any difference what I said, or what anyone said, what she wanted was retribution. My soft skills were useless. Looking her in the eye and positive body language wouldn't help. I looked her dog in the eye instead, smiling, thinking at least she doesn't take it out on you.

Just as she was drawing breath for another rant the all-clear came over the radio and at the same time a train could be heard approaching the station. Although we had spoken for only a few minutes I felt angry and ill-used. A devil on my shoulder speculated, would I get away with shoving her in front of the arriving train? Where were the platform video cameras pointing? How hard would it be to snatch the lead at the same time to save the innocent dog? With these homicidal thoughts I wished her a good day and retreated. She screamed, '*I really don't like your tone,*' at an empty space, the space I had been standing in and had now vacated, and then, still bristling like a bar brawler who cannot land a punch, she boarded the train.

(11)

It is profoundly true that the speed at which we live our lives affects how we perceive everything around us. A conjuror learns to move very quickly, while distracting attention away from the sleight of hand. However successful the distraction, there is a speed below which the sleight will re-materialise and be noticeable. Various activities and ways of thinking can only be successful if they are organised and performed slowly enough to operate without omissions, perceptual and practical. There is a speed above which the task or thought breaks down.

We currently lead lives based on the assumption that anything that may be speeded up, should be. Accelerated is best, will lead to an enhancement of efficiency. This approach rests on a failure to understand that some things need to be done slowly. A new oven combines microwaves and jets of super-heated air and will roast a chicken in under four minutes. Am I alone in feeling that the hour or so of slowly roasting chicken aromas is one of the best things about roast chicken? Will this now come in an aerosol?

A man running a race so slowly he is in last place, is heckled by someone in the crowd. 'Come on, slow coach! You're last! Get a move on!' 'I may be last in this race,' says the runner, 'but I'm way out ahead in the next one.'

(12)

Another blind customer, this time a man, with a white cane but no dog. He was softly spoken and asked to be helped, if this was possible, to Platform 1, as he was on his way to Marble Arch. He asked in a mild yet cultivated voice. I recognised his accent as Egyptian and wondered if I should use the Arabic I had learned dealing in oriental carpets and rugs in the Arabian Gulf. He held on to my arm gently and through the point of contact I had the strangest impression of strength and inappropriate perception, as if through lightly touching me he was evaluating what I was like, the tactile equivalent of a hard stare. It felt like being scanned with sensors, like an alien vessel meeting the Enterprise in *Star Trek*.

As we approached the platform I made small talk and the blind Egyptian responded gracefully and all at once I realised that he was, seemingly, replying to questions I had formed in my mind, but not yet asked. He could not be anticipating them from my earlier remarks, the thoughts were unconnected, followed no logical sequence. I had encountered this sort of thing before, knew its 'taste,' but did not expect it here and in the ordinary course of my duties.

The train was pulling into the station as this realisation dawned on me and I had no time to take it up with him, or to ask a significant question. He thanked me profusely for guiding him as I handed him on to the train. I have tried hard but now cannot remember what we spoke about or even what he looked like. However, I can remember two things: that he wore a green necktie, and that as the train pulled out of the station a pale white butterfly hovered momentarily in the place he had been standing, then flew away down the platform, over the heads of the crowds. I noticed that no one looked up and it passed unseen until I too lost sight of it.

(13)

It is possible to rank the senses in an order where we might more readily accept that what we are experiencing may not be real. So, for example, something heard is, in a way, frequently regarded as less real to us than, say, something seen. In fact, sight is the sense most of us would place at the top of the list, optical illusions and doubting Thomases notwithstanding. Our visual assumptions have yielded proverbial expressions such as 'a picture is worth a thousand words' and 'seeing is believing'.

Experimental research has convincingly demonstrated that the sense of sight, no more or less than our other senses, operates as a censor, allowing through only certain visual information out of which the brain constructs the visible world. In order to process an otherwise overwhelming amount of data, the visual cortex 'best guesses' so that certain visual impressions will be seen not as they really are, but as something they nearly resemble.

So when we say, 'I'll believe it when I see it,' we might reasonably reverse this, and instead declare, 'I'll see this when I believe it.'

(14)

On duty in the Bullring, the main ticket concourse located immediately below the Oxford Circus crossroads, I flexed my universal gatepass while waiting for the next puzzled traveller to stop so I could offer assistance. Unlike any of my colleagues, I enjoyed approaching people as soon as they hesitated, typically gazing at the small free underground plan or map, searching for an answer to their question 'Where now?'

Bouncing around, like a pinball, kept me amused and energised and contrasted with the slower pace suited to the world below, which seemed composed of another element inhibiting speed, slowing motion, like swimming in an aquarium. Many of my co-workers were committed to an endless search for an ideal spot suited to whiling away the hours with as few interruptions as possible, preferably somewhere where you could comfortably lean or sit and rest your feet, while avoiding Supervisors and the incessant demands of the travelling public.

An otherwise nondescript man, wearing glasses, attracts my attention. As soon as he passes through the barriers he pushes his myopic milk-bottle lenses on to the top of his head and, rummaging in his jacket pocket, plucks out a telescope. Extending the telescope he peers with tremendous concentration at the signs above each of the descending escalators. Letters six-inches high indicate the way to reach the three Tube lines which intersect at Oxford Circus. They are hard to miss unless you are very short-sighted indeed. He scans the signs, like someone searching among the details of a far-off horizon, focuses on the words 'Central Line', de-telescopes his optical prop and then marches confidently off in the direction he has discovered without anyone's help. This man, although afflicted, had come prepared.

(15)

The most essential gift for a good writer is a built-in, shock proof shit detector. This is the writer's radar and all great writers have had it.
ERNEST HEMINGWAY

Jeff, like me a part-time SA, complains whenever we see each other that his part-time earnings are falling short of what he needs to get by. I knew it had a lot to do with the other topic we always talk about: how much it is possible to drink in a single evening and how to avoid the risk of a snap drugs and alcohol test. He chews mints all the time to outwit the General Station Manager who has developed the unnerving habit of standing inches from your face making small talk while he secretly sniffs your breath for the telltale scent of booze.

Jeff's income-boosting schemes were often bizarre. He had seen a newspaper advert soliciting volunteers for a nutritional research programme. It offered £50 for what appeared to be two weeks of keeping a brief diary of diet. Sending for an information pack he learned he'd have to attend a medical, be measured and weighed and pronounced free of infections. They would supply a sophisticated electronic weighing machine to weigh all his food and would also provide receptacles for his stools. Not stool samples, but for all his stools over a ten-day period. The survey was focusing on the normal bowel habits of healthy people and needed to get a toilet bowl perspective, as it were, of what came out, trusting you to record faithfully what went in. I had friends who had raised money *in extremis* by selling blood and, in one case, by selling sperm to an artificial insemination donor clinic in Helsinki. But selling shit at £50 for a whole lot was, I thought, a curious idea.

Jeff wanted the £50, but couldn't face accumulating faeces for ten days and then delivering it all to the University of the South Bank. He also felt suspicious of the three capsules of *inert material* they wanted him to swallow on days 1 to 3, 'to help us track your digestive progress'. It sounded like a radioactive tracer and even for the hard-up Jeff £50 wasn't enough to risk cancer of the bowel.

'Just make up the diary stuff,' I said, 'don't bother weighing anything. As for the stools, just gather whatever you can find in your local park. Twenty kilos of dog shit, formerly Pedigree Chum but now claimed to be the human output of a macrobiotic vegetarian diet, should keep any researcher in grant money for a tidy while trying to figure it out. Just think' I continued, '£50 for a walk round the park with a shovel, and at the same time you'd be doing your civic duty scooping up dog poop for free. Everyone wins!' We both laughed, knowing he wouldn't do it.

(16)

At dinner parties it quickly became clear that my ideas about bending 'unnecessary' rules differed from those of most of the other guests. Advising someone who wanted to teach English in Japan that a TEFL qualification was useful and having established that he felt confident that he could actually teach English, I told him he should just print up a certificate, as attending a real course was boring and expensive. Two other guests, both barristers, bristled, but said nothing. I pointed out that the Japanese were very reluctant to check foreign qualifications, partly because they felt unconfident about their English, the language they would need to write in to make such an enquiry. It was, I thought, a nice paradox.

A friend of mine needed some medicine in India and was unwilling to go to a doctor. He went into a pharmacy and simply asked for what he wanted, but was refused and told to get a doctor's prescription. Going round the corner he found a rubber stamp shop, instantly had a stamp made up in his name indicating he was now a fully qualified medical doctor. He took the stamp back to the pharmacy, asked for a piece of paper, stamped it and wrote out and signed a prescription for the medicine. The pharmacist, not troubled in any way by the transformation of patient into doctor, having obtained a 'prescription' was now happy to oblige.

We hear of cases of all sorts of professionals who are finally unmasked as not having the qualifications they claimed on getting their positions; in one case a 'surgeon' had been working successfully in a hospital for six years before he was found out. No one he operated on had died. His procedures, although self-taught, were orthodox. None of his qualified colleagues could tell that he was a 'fraud'.

Considering a painting which, until it was declared a fake, had drawn crowds of admirers but was now unable to attract a single visitor, I ask myself: if the picture has not changed, what has?

(17)

'Guess what?' said Deputy Dawg, the name by which we referred to Derek Davies, a Duty Station Manager, whose speech was slurred like the cartoon dog. 'What?' I replied, realising that the chance of nipping round the corner to buy a decent cup of coffee was fading with each minute remaining to me before my official start. 'John Prescott, you know, the Deputy Prime

Minister . . .' Yes, I knew of John Prescott and that he was the Deputy Prime Minister. 'He's passing through Oxo and will arrive on your platform this morning.'

I could hardly contain my excitement, but as everyone else seemed keyed up by the through-put of a VIP I feigned a small degree of interest, 'What time will he be here?' 'At about 8.50,' said Deputy Dawg. 'Good,' I improvised, 'that just gives me time for a bite of breakfast and a cup of coffee. I need to be on the ball with the Deputy Prime Minister visiting.' I backed out of the Ops Room and left at the double to obtain my breakfast before anyone told me to stay put.

I carried my sandwich into the Staff Mess Room feeling pleased with myself and quickly ate it. The coffee I took into the Ops Room, feeling safe to drink it in front of a manager while he was distracted briefing me about the VIP visit.

I was to make sure that, in addition to myself, the two members of staff on the Central Line platforms had extension mikes, so we could all make clear announcements to impress the delegation. Prescott probably couldn't give a damn about Tube announcements, but he would be travelling with the Managing Director of London Underground and the Head of the Central Line. He would also be met by our hated General Station Manager who had the power to make those with immediate authority over me very unhappy, so it was a Level 1 alert!

Calmed by the coffee I asked for a clean hi-vi; mine was always grubby as I refused to wash it, it was the way I reminded myself that the air down in the tunnels was nearly unfit to breathe. When the orange vest was completely black it would be time to quit, to seek out the light and fresh air of the world above. I gave my scruffy boots a quick working over with some toilet roll, straightened my appalling polyester clip-on tie and looked in the small mirror above the sink to see whether my unironed and very wrinkled white non-uniformed shirt was mostly covered up by the orange reflective vest.

It was the first time I had tried to smarten up and it would have to do. I descended to Platform 6, telling a couple of buskers encountered on the way to push off to avoid the Police Security Blanket we had been assured would descend on us prior to Prescott's arrival.

About half an hour later the Police Security Blanket arrived. It consisted of a stout British Transport Police Sergeant without a hi-vi and a pretty blonde WPC with an outsized truncheon dangling from her shapely hip. They nodded hello and went round the corner. Perhaps they were walking the route, checking for assassins or for banana skins.

A strange frenzy had developed on Platform 6. Three cleaners, the entire station's on-duty contingent, were busy cleaning an already clean platform. Their Supervisor, Mr James, a jovial and rotund West African, was himself armed with a polishing rag and seemed to be scrubbing the wall opposite the spot where John Prescott's carriage was predicted to halt. I told an Egyptian friend about this and she said, 'It's just like home!'

Prescott's train pulled into the platform and everything was ready. Or almost everything, as one half of the Police Security Blanket – the Tubby Sergeant – came round the corner to ask me if the Deputy Prime Minister would be travelling in the driver's cab. I told him that he had already arrived, pointing down the platform to the slowly moving party of suits. 'Oops!' said the highly trained bobby, slipping quickly round the corner to his appointed position.

I made a careful announcement over the PA system, in well-paced BBC English. I realised it must sound odd on the otherwise colloquially dominated Tube to hear the lengthened vowels of received pronunciation, but it's my voice.

The party snaked its way down the platform towards the point where they would turn and make their way to the Central Line. Prescott was at the head, with the General Station Manager greasily hovering at his elbow. As Prescott came level with me he looked away, deliberately avoiding eye contact, ignoring my smiling nod in lieu of saluting, which despite my being in uniform seemed a ridiculous thing to do. He was a dwarfish man, with a face like a frog. The heavy bags under his eyes imparted a degree of weariness to his every gesture and strongly reminded me of the comedian Les Dawson. But the illusion was unconvincing, no one was laughing.

(18)

We tend to behave oddly around those who are famous. Why is this? Are we anticipating an advantage should we find favour with those who may be placed to intercede on our behalf in something we want to do or obtain? Do we think that fame is connected with the worth of the person so honoured? The twentieth century has yielded a category previously unknown: those who are famous for being famous. They have no great skills. They cannot sing and do not make us laugh. They are not athletes whom we might seek to emulate, nor are they especially intelligent or wise. They may be wealthy or beautiful – but these attributes hardly seem to explain their fame, as other beautiful and wealthy individuals are completely unknown.

(19)

A naked man running endless circuits around the Bullring is finally approached by Mike Murphy, an Irish Supervisor with thinning red hair and a superdry sense of humour. Holding on to the man's bare arm he waits for a colleague to bring out an abandoned coat which he knows is hanging in the Supervisors' office. The garment is a lime green fleecy tracksuit top, with a Lost Property label dangling from it, and he hands it to the naked man, as an improvised cover for his private parts. Not understanding, the naked man puts his arms in the sleeves and then pulls on the top, and is now naked only from the waist down. He is escorted to the Police Room to await the arrival of the British Transport Police and where Mike waits with him, nervously as this is a new experience with unwelcome dimensions. 'Why did you take your clothes off?' asks Mike, to fill the growing silence in the small room. 'Jesus told me to.'

(20)

Every morning an achondroplastic dwarf in a pin-striped suit and carrying a full-sized attaché case arrives on Platform 6 and marches past me. I wonder about his suit which is smart, of good cloth and finely stitched. Does it cost less than a regularly sized made-to-measure suit as it uses less cloth; or more, as the small pattern has to be specially cut and particularly close stitching is required? Is there a specialist clothes shop for dwarfs, like High & Mighty for the very tall and the stout? After a few days of smiling and nodding at each other I ask him. His clothes are made for him by a friend. She is a fashion student. Later he tells me they are getting married. Seeking a solution to what to wear he found a wife. She is of normal stature and, he confides, they hope to have full-sized babies.

(21)

There is smoke pouring from the running rails on my platform and I raise the alarm. It is enjoyable to blast the metal with the white foam of a AFFF extinguisher and, while fully justified by the situation, it still retains a sense of the illicit. (Does a soldier feel the same way when he shoots someone under orders?) A train has been stopped half way down the platform to act as protection and Barry Glover hangs off the front of the train, stretching out acrobatically to obtain a new angle for a further spraying of foam. When the train has gone we scan the tracks with a thermal imaging device. Heat shows on the small screen of the gadget as a brightness and we confirm that the rails register no residual heat. Part of the tradition of this piece of technology is that it must be trained on any women standing on the platform. The heat-indicating brightness on a human female highlights heads and – the point of the exercise – crotches. An angry woman storming off after complaining about the delays is scanned as an afterthought. She is not hot-headed as I expected but, like the undead showing no reflection in a mirror, hardly registers signs of being alive at all.

(22)

A colleague, like me an SA, who works mostly at our sister station, Holborn, is the improbably named John Major. We have met only once or twice when I learn that he has successfully retired on medical grounds. A sum of money by way of compensation for an accident is spoken of in envious tones in the Mess Room, as if it is an achievement really worth trying to emulate. The story is that in some unexplained fashion his locker had fallen, with him beneath it, causing unspecified injuries. This passes into the oral lore of Oxford Circus as the Collapse of John Major's Cabinet.

(23)

No mind is much employed upon the present; recollection and anticipation fill up almost all our moments.

SAMUEL JOHNSON

'It's been much longer than a minute. It said the next one's due in a minute. Over a minute ago it said that – and it's still not here. The train. How long's a minute, then?' The squat man I watched timing the overhead dot matrix indicator board against the second hand of his Swatch spoke to me in a hostile and harassed tone. 'You see, it's not an absolute minute,' I explained. 'It's relative to other events and becomes inaccurate if, for example, a moving train stops and before this delay is uploaded into the system.' He looked at me as if I was mad. Or just too stupid to understand that a minute is a minute whatever anyone says.

(24)

Time. Time waits for no man. Time flies. A watched pot never boils. We have endless proverbial expressions and wise saws about the subjective nature of time. But the point about proverbs seems to be that, once stated, they can be forgotten and in this way sometimes operate to erase the significance of their messages.

That time is subjective however accurate the watch you are wearing may, in consequence, be forgotten fact. Two minutes in a boiling bath will, if experienced, convince you of the subjective impression that it seems to last longer than an hour in the park with a lover drinking chilled white wine against a background of summer sounds. But experiences do not often crop up juxtaposed so as to cement this understanding in our minds.

(25)

Whoever gives advice to a heedless man
is himself in need of advice.
SAADI

I was trying to convince my friend and colleague Phil Morton that he would be better off working than skiving; that dodging tasks made the day drag. He disagreed and revealed that a better way to shorten the tedium of work was to alter your state of consciousness. The best way to do this, he said, was to find a safe place to sleep.

He had found a cupboard which could be closed and opened from the inside. There was a small wooden platform stored inside, designed for standing on to enhance the perspective of platform staff on a busy platform, but hardly ever used. He could comfortably sit on this. It was necessary to switch off the light inside the cupboard as it could be seen from outside through the gap between the door and the frame and also to turn off his radio to prevent telltale bleeps which might be heard and traced by a passing Supervisor. For Phil his day was a success if he could spend time asleep in the dark, in radio silence, in a cupboard in a tunnel one hundred feet below a London street and be paid for it.

(26)

We are alive and well, yet enslaved and ignorant of our situation. Possessing the capacity to realise the truth of this assertion is the hope of mankind. 'Realise the truth' does not, however, mean come to agree with this statement or be persuaded by argument. Rather it refers to undergoing experiences so that perceptive capacities are 'revived' and that, by reference to such perceptions, the truth is known directly.

The prison metaphor says much about our situation but, unlike a real gaol, in our prison the walls, bars, cells and guards are disguised. We see the boundaries of our cells as either inevitable or as serving a necessary function. The bars protect us; the guards guarantee our safety. We are suffering from a prison psychosis, where everything we think must in some way be related to our prison worldview. This includes such ideas as: there is nothing beyond the prison, so we might as well settle down and make the best of it. That our activities and even our pleasures are subject to prison rules – and are highly attenuated – does not occur to us.

We have evolved a prison language in which it is nearly impossible to describe accurately life outside the prison. Prisoners who manage to approach the question of escape often do so in a manner which renders escape impossible; as if, for example, a group of prisoners were to petition the prison authorities for approval of their escape plans in order to predict whether an attempt is worthwhile. A preparation for escape is necessary, where the idea can be established that prison reality is a distortion and cannot form the basis for living in the outside world. A condition for such a preparatory orientation is waiting for the right society of inmates in the same cell block at an opportune time.

(27)

How many times did someone say to me 'I cannot find the way out. Why are there no signs?' There were eighteen Way Out signs on or near my platform, but they might as well have been invisible. What they were asking for was to be shown or led out by someone who knew the way. And to be soothed and reassured that it was indeed impossible to get out alone.

(28)

There were eight shopping days left until Christmas, but the shabby black youth making his way down the escalator to the northbound Bakerloo Line platform didn't know or care about this. He was sleeping rough and shopping wasn't a priority, Christmas only a child-hood memory. His head was spinning. He didn't know how much more of this he could take. It had grown colder in the last few days and earlier he couldn't feel his toes. He couldn't smell his own stench but, like the wind made visible by the motion of leaves and trees, recognised its existence from the way those around him inched away. He was muttering rhythmically to himself, 'Don't think, don't think,' over and over again.

At nearly 11 p.m. the young man stood, not quite upright, on the platform crowded with homebound Lon-doners, most of whom were in high spirits, had been drinking, and were talking too loudly, but none of whom noticed how their exuberance further depressed the down-hearted lone figure. How it emphasised his exclusion, like laughter in the next room. A room you cannot enter. Looking up he gazed at a poster. A beauti-ful girl selling something for £19.99. Might as well be £1,999, he thought – and when was the last time a beautiful girl looked at him as anything other than an object to hurry past. His head was spinning faster now and for some reason his heartbeat had quickened. The thoughts chased each other round, like rubbish swirling in an empty doorway. Keep them spinning, don't let the thoughts rise to the top . . . don't think, don't think . . .

A loud but familiar noise cut into his consciousness; the train was approaching. He shuffled forwards as if moving to board the train. Don't think, just do it, like the Nike ad. He smiled. The train had yet to arrive, was only beginning to pull into the platform as the young man stepped out into space directly in front of the oncoming train's headlights. His suddenly illuminated body flew forwards from where the driver gazed in horror, slamming on the brakes by reflex not thought; or sideways from the viewpoint of the woman who screamed. No one heard the noise of the impact, like a television image with the sound turned down. The body fell out of sight as the train stopped suddenly, three and a half carriages into the platform. Someone hit the emergency blue button of the Help Point next to where the body (he had, in the minds of those close enough to see, changed from a person into a 'body') had disappeared under the train. Two SAs, patrolling in pairs for company and conversation, slowly walked on to the platform to see why a train had stopped; they didn't know about the body yet and moved with the usual slowly-does-it pace of a normal evening.

Almost at once the Control Room and Supervisors knew there was a one-under; what I heard called in New York a track pizza. All the necessary calls were made; police, emergency services and the Underground hierarchy were notified. Drama fizzed in the air, it was a life and death situation more meaningful than the run-of-the-mill day's non-events – stalled trains, lost tickets, tourists' wallets expertly picked – but there were still passengers arriving on the platform unaware of the body beneath the leading carriage of the stopped train. 'Come on, mate, move this train, I want to get home tonight not tomorrow,' shouted an overweight man wearing a woolly football hat that made him look like a simpleton or a Belgian peasant condemned to damnation in a Bruegel painting. Another man was tapping on the driver's window. Inside, the driver didn't hear, but kept rocking slowly back and forth, refusing to come out or to talk to anyone. He was in shock, didn't know enough to be able to work out who was to 'blame'.

Didn't even know for sure that the body beneath his wheels was dead. Sometimes they didn't die: like the would-be suicide who lost both arms and both legs but survived to a life many would argue was not worth living. And then, all at once, a density of whispers and shouts made everyone realise that someone had died and a hush descended. Newcomers were silenced by those who knew. The seriousness of death had exerted itself.

Two Supervisors, Harish Choudhury and Old Tom, arrived to take over. Old Tom went to the opposite end of the platform and, refusing to come near the train or the body, pretended to be occupied on his radio. Harish would only look at the body through his hands in front of his face, visibly upset and fearing weeks of nightmares of a decapitated or mutilated corpse. But the body was intact and resembled someone sleeping. When the paramedics had confirmed he was dead, one joked to Old Tom about the body still being warm as he accompanied the body-bag and its contents to the surface. 'Here,' he said, unzipping it a few inches, 'why don't you feel and see?'

(29)

What is this life if, full of care,
we have no time to stand and stare?
W. H. DAVIES

In the morning, standing on the neighbouring platform, I was shown the exact spot where the young man had died fewer than twelve hours earlier. I thought I could see a trace of blood, but it was only a KitKat wrapper, discarded on the scattered sand. Something drew me to return to this spot again and again throughout the morning, as if trying to surprise an ellusive clue as to why someone might choose to die in this sad place.

Next day, chatting to a Bakerloo driver I mention the incident. He tells me he knows the driver involved; he has been given compassionate leave. 'Lucky bastard!' he says, assuming we are all the same, that we all want to be paid without having to work, 'Wish it had been me!' But I didn't believe him.

(30)

In 1960 Peter Llewelyn Davies, the publisher and brother of Barrie's inspiration for Peter Pan, jumped in front of a train at Sloane Square. The papers predictably headlined, 'Peter Pan's Last Flight'; 'Boy Who Couldn't Grow Up Dead'. There are, on average, two jumpers a week system-wide and a special squad exists to clean up the mess and get things moving as quickly as possible. Small boys were for ever asking if they would die if they touched the rails. I told them they would roast at once, end up like a piece of Kentucky Fried Chicken.

(31)

Usually between 9.30 and 10 a.m. I would grow restless and feel like wandering away from Platform 6 for a change of scenery. Most of my colleagues whose rush-hour platform duties, unlike mine which were fixed, only lasted four days at a time, would take a cigarette or coffee break at about 9.45, sometimes asking on the radio for a PNR (Personal Needs Relief), sometimes just chancing non-detection by anyone who might object.

I felt better going upstairs around 10.10 or 10.15, taking five minutes to wash my face and extract some of the grime from my nostrils and hands, and then wandering over to the Ops Room for a cup of tea and a few minutes off my feet, before turning the escalators around at 10.30.

Oxford Circus uses the Main Ticketing Hall, or the Bullring, as an entrance and exit system during the rush-hour but after 10.30 a.m. transforms this part of the station into a one-way entrance-only system. Implementing this is known as the turn-around. A number of up escalators are reversed to travel down, so that there is only one rather than two ways out from either the Bakerloo or Victoria lines; the Central Line exits remain unchanged, always leading to Argyle Street.

(32)

From Platform 6 I wander down the steps following the signed route to the Central Line, past the weeping wall, where water slowly seeps through every day and night of the year, and along the long passageway. Halfway down is a favourite site for buskers and I would sometimes go there to listen to the music and occasionally to enjoy it.

Generally, the standard of musicianship required of a successful busker is not high. Most buskers play the same 20 to 30-second extract from something recognisable over and over again. 'Streets of London'. 'Wonderwall'. Anything by Bob Marley. Or, if the busker is a classical musician, an extract from a suite or concerto that you might find any day on Classic FM but, as on that station, never the entire piece. From time to time I was surprised: once a black flautist from Mali playing 'Martin menoit son porceau' – a sixteenth-century French bawdy song by Claudin de Sermisy, telling of the unnatural passion of a farmer for his pig, which seemed a bizarre choice for a Muslim; another time a tall Chinese student singing without accompaniment a lyric poem of the Sung Dynasty. The melodious classical Mandarin was rendered into English on copies of a CD of his singing he had propped against the wall. I picked one up and read:

> High in green mansions
> curtain shadows
> won't block away melancholy,
> same mood as last year
> on the same day

Round the corner I saw the singer's friend, another Chinese whom, from his demeanour, I also took to be a student. He was sitting on the floor studying a book with a look of intense concentration on his smooth face, milk-bottle glasses balanced on the end of his nose. I positioned myself so that I might glance at the front cover, might discover what he was studying with such close attention and, after a few seconds, not looking up or noticing me, as he moved into a more comfortable position, I was rewarded: Jeffrey Archer's *A Twist in the Tale*.

(33)

The official policy on busking was that it was strictly forbidden. Buskers all knew this, but simply ignored it, often setting up under signs warning of £100 fines. In practice there was a more flexible approach. A buskers' site would, nearby, be marked by a poster with dates, times and initials scratched in a dozen hands at head height. It was, of course, a rota. Although sometimes someone who was new or just desperate would cheat and write their own details falsely to lay claim to an already booked slot of time, there was no protection racket. It was something that this didn't occur on the Tube and I wondered why.

Buskers are thought of as free spirits, as individualists, but from my observation they seemed to be creatures of habit like the rest of us. Once a pitch is shown to be lucrative, they will return to it like going to the office every day. At Oxo the regulars were grudgingly tolerated as they sat reading or listening to a Walkman in the cross passageways, with their guitars and amplifiers or sometimes something larger, like a double bass in its case, stacked to one side while they waited for lunchtime and a better flow of punters.

I watched for signs of a stooge, like a street trader's plant, someone who just went in circles putting coins into the busker's open guitar case, riding up and down the escalators. There is nothing quite like social proof for priming the generosity pump – he gives, I give, she gives, we all give – but I never saw it. Perhaps buskers have yet to achieve the sophistication of the hawkers of perfectly packed but heavily diluted designer perfumes who lurked above ground selling their counterfeit wares.

(34)

On the westbound Central Line platform there were more passengers than usual for this time of day, a time when the morning rush-hour normally slackened a little. I glanced automatically at the dot matrix indicator board, before remembering that it did not work, and saw it was impotently attempting to distract away from its wounded state with repeated warnings that pick-pockets were known to work this station. I looked down the tunnel towards Tottenham Court Road but there was no train; when a train is coming you can see its headlights reflected on the running rails long before you see the headlights themselves. I saw no lights but, strangely, noticed something was moving.

I walked down the platform, past the vacant staring crowds, away from the headwall for a better look. The vision soon resolved into a figure walking next to the wall, down the tunnel, towards me. He or she was not wearing a hi-vi reflector vest, or carrying a lamp or anything which might indicate membership of the Underground about some official business. The figure, by now clearly a man, was walking quite quickly and after a minute or two he came alongside the platform and heaved himself up at a single bound. I had been watching nervously for signs of a train, although I knew the Line Controller had been informed of what was hap-pening and had suspended the line.

He was a young man, perhaps early twenties, wear-ing a sort of shell suit with a hood, which he had pulled over his head. The jacket had a Nike 'tick' logo on the front. I walked up to him and said, 'What on earth are you doing?' He stared at me, his large brown eyes twinkling oddly, and said very slowly that he was in a hurry, had asked a man dressed like me when the next train would arrive, only to be told that it was probably faster to walk. So he had. His voice was deliberate and slurred, not from drink, but from something hard-wired. He put me in mind of Steinbeck's Lennie. Having explained to his own satisfaction he walked on, past me, towards the exits. His receding broad back bore the slogan 'Just Do It!' I didn't follow him. There didn't seem anything more to say.

(35)

Although my nostrils became caked with soot within a few minutes of breathing normally in the tunnels, I hadn't noticed any diminution in my sense of smell. It was a sense I had come to respect after a blow on the head in Japan had the unexpected side-effect of dramatically sharpening my olfactory capacities. I was surprised to be able to enter a room and detect the recent presence of a friend from faint traces of the shampoo he preferred, which no one else could smell. I could also now smell changes in the weather, accurately predicting the coming of rain and snow, like a mariner or shepherd.

I began to take this for granted and grew used to sniffing the air like a bloodhound and believing I could follow a trail. Perhaps fortuitously and heading off my new career as a weather prophet, after a few months this heightened sense began to fade to more normal dimensions. But it had made me more aware and I believe I have retained an unusually acute sense of smell. I have come to value smells, scents and aromas actively and to interrogate them for nuances; looking for clues not yielded up by other primary senses, the modern ones we rely upon more than we should. You might well be able to smell something you cannot see or hear. You can even smell stuff not normally acknowledged as within this sense register and I came to believe I could, quite literally, smell a lie.

(36)

On a train to Nakamurabashi, it was nearly midnight, and I was tired and already thinking about unrolling my futon and crawling beneath the warm quilt. The next day I had no early morning appointments and might have a lie-in. The train was not as full as it often was at this time. It wasn't the last train, but the system would soon shut down.

A schoolgirl was seated diagonally across from me. She had on her sailor suit uniform. As we stopped at a station a middle-aged salaryman staggered into the train just as the doors were shutting. His tie was pulled down and he had a bright red face, the face of a certain type of inebriated Japanese.

The man sat next to the girl, although there were many other seats free, with much more space for him to sprawl. Soon he swayed into the sleeping position assumed by most of my fellow passengers. But he was not sleeping; he was preparing a plausible assault on his neighbour. Sliding forwards, he suddenly sat up and then, like a stop-action film, fell slowly sideways so that his head came to rest on the schoolgirl's navy-skirted lap. I looked at her face. It had the unmistakable rictus of the truly terrified. She did not know how to escape, a stoat caught in the headlights of an oncoming vehicle.

I wondered if she would move. I knew she would

not thank me for intervening. I'll give her a little more time to act, I thought, but if he starts to grope her . . . My senses were acute and I had already mentally calculated how to lock his arm so that he would come quietly and not attempt to fight; and recalled the Japanese for train pervert, *chikan*. I watched and listened and distinctly heard him sniff. Not the sniff of an office worker with a cold. It was the deep draft of inwardly drawn breath of the lecher whose nose is presently, miraculously, only inches from the private parts of a schoolgirl.

It was enough for the girl to snap out of her paralysis. She slid sideways and twisted 180 degrees to her feet, using the momentum of the slowing train. Standing she moved down the train and took another seat. The sniffer-*chikan* lay where he had fallen, pretending to sleep.

(37)

The worst possible time for anything to go wrong was during the rush-hour, not an hour but roughly a period of nearly two hours between 8.30 and 10.15 a.m.

The signed route to the Central Line led past the weeping or crying wall. This was a section of the passageway which was subject to a continuous low level of water seepage. Engineers had long tried to get at the problem, using caulking and insulating materials to little effect. The pumps – Oxford Circus like all tunnel section stations was obliged to pump out water all day and night – sometimes failed and when this happened the crying wall became inconsolable and gushed buckets.

In the same corridor, there was now water leaking out of an overhead light socket, so that anyone looking up at the wrong moment and yawning might get an unwelcome drip filtered through quantities of unknown filth, with unknowable and possibly serious health risks. We had reluctantly decided at 8 a.m. to close this route to the Central Line, redirecting passengers another way.

(38)

There are two of us standing there and we have written an explanation on a whiteboard for those who prefer their information free of human contact. Streams of passengers, many of whom always travel on the same part of the train, always crossing the platform at the same point, automatically descending the same stairs and pounding along the same passageways, were about to be shocked out of autopilot. They would need to assess unexpected information, unwelcome information, which at first they would, perhaps justifiably, suppose could only affect their journey for the worse.

(39)

For most of us the mental starting point of a shock is always expectation; a form of living in the immediate future, rather than the present; an unwarranted presumption that everything should turn out just as you want it to – and if it doesn't you *rightly* begin to feel upset. The expectation in such cases is the presumed right that, say, a journey to work will be trouble-free and will resemble more or less precisely the journey of yesterday. An odd thought, when put this way.

The next mental quirk clearly on display is that of

making judgements on insufficient information. You walk around the corner and see a passageway to another Underground line closed by a barrier and members of staff standing there. You assume that this means the line you wish to connect to, possibly the only straightforward way of reaching your destination, is not running. *This is intolerable as I am already late.* So you show your anger. Shout. Swear. Even jump up and down like a cartoon figure, and it's easy to imagine steam coming out of your ears. This is living not in the future or the present, but in the past: you have perhaps seen corridors barriered off in this way before and on those occasions it meant that the line reached this way was not running, so you assume the same is true once again. It takes little effort to verify this, but you are too pissed off to do so.

Or you walk up to the member of staff and spit out your feelings of betrayal and irritation in an insulting quasi-question about what's up. This varies from 'What the fuck now?', a question obvious in its meaning, but only reluctantly answered by someone who has just calmly explained how to reach the Central Line to 4,000 people in the last half an hour on an individual basis, smiling for the first 1,756 encounters, to 'You call this a service? This isn't a rail service, *this* is *a joke*.'

(40)

A middle-aged man walks round the corner. Spotting us, he turns red at an alarming rate, grimaces, all but foams at the mouth and flings his briefcase against the wall as if he has no more use for it. The catch is sprung and some papers and an apple fall out. He is saying the word 'fuck' over and over again, like the mantras used by Californian cults which encourage chanting for what you want.

After a couple of dozen more 'fucks' he retrieves his battered briefcase, scoops up the fallen papers and retraces his steps to Platform 6. We have redirected another twenty or so people during this outburst, but he seems not to be listening. He does not speak to us or trouble to learn that the Central Line is fine and that it can be reached simply and more rapidly by an alternative route. And as his heaving shoulders disappear around the corner, I see he has left his apple behind too.

(41)

Marcus Aurelius, the Roman Emperor and Stoic philosopher, advised that we should begin each day by telling ourselves: Today I shall be meeting with interference, ingratitude, insolence, disloyalty, ill-will and selfishness – all of them due to the offenders' ignorance of what is good or evil. But for my part I have long perceived the nature of good and its nobility, the nature of evil and its meanness, and also the nature of the culprit himself, who is my brother (not in the physical sense, but as a fellow creature similarly endowed with reason and a share of the divine); therefore none of these things can injure me, for nobody can implicate me in what is degrading. Neither can I be angry with my brother or fall foul of him; for he and I were born to work together, like a man's two hands, feet, or eyelids, or like the upper and lower rows of his teeth. To obstruct each other is against Nature's law – and what is irritation or aversion but a form of obstruction?

(42)

I differ from my colleague in wishing to explain in detail why the passageway is barriered. Yet I recognise you have to deliver such information in a very truncated form, at a pace which matches the flow of passengers. A curt 'Up the stairs and turn right' would have mystified me and so I tried something a little longer: 'Just the passageway . . . to reach the Central Line, follow the Way Out signs to the escalators, don't go up the escalators . . . follow the signs to the Central Line . . . the Central Line's fine, it's just the passageway . . . it's flooded . . .'

Try repeating this continuously for two hours, with only the occasional break to answer someone asking, 'What the fuck?' or 'Call this a railway?'

(43)

If you work in the House of A,
do not expect to get paid by B.
SAADI

I had just spent the second half of my morning chasing off the slattern-plus-baby gangs of Irish travellers who besiege the tunnels of Oxford Circus and some of the surrounding stations begging. We were their patch and moving them along was a normal chore, but sometimes it depressed me. I had nothing against begging, but regarded professional begging by the devious able as doubly disagreeable: it was not justifiable in itself and, worse still, it served to inoculate the general public against lending some small measure of support to the genuinely cast down and friendless.

And, of course, there was the question of the children used as props to pick the sympathy pockets of any naïve passers-by: starved or pinched to cry, or drugged or, at best, given quantities of sweets and slaps to keep them still and quiet, they were daily forced to breathe polluted air for hours and hours whenever their 'mothers' chose to beg. After five or ten minutes under ground, blowing my nose always yielded an unpleasant black scum of unidentifiable particulate matter.

There was also something ridiculous about how we dealt with them. We were not allowed to touch them to detain or arrest them, and if they spotted a member of staff approaching they would normally jump up and try to hide. This led to chases. The only Gaelic insult I knew – *Pogue Mahoan!* (Kiss my arse!) – was my battle cry as I tore after the disappearing hordes, co-ordinating a pincer movement on the radio.

Picture, if you will, a gang of overweight sluttish women, running full tilt with pushchairs loaded with soiled and drooling infants, fleeing along the subterranean corridors of the Tube, screaming abuse at their pursuers, being chased for the most part by fit young men obliged to try their best to herd them on a train, any train will do, and out of their station, following orders to behave like sheep dogs dispatching an unwanted flock.

(44)

One morning a teenage girl wearing a headscarf, multi-layered flowery long skirts and cheap coat more usually seen on the streets of Sophia or Belgrade walked up to me on Platform 6. She handed me a scrap of paper.

Scraps of paper handed over like this were usually addresses their possessors were seeking but did not know how to find. I have even been shown addresses in other cities, other countries, by those journeying via airports or railway stations. But this was not an address other than in the sense of a plea. It said, 'I am from Romania. I have no money. Please help.' I took out a fountain pen, wrote 'No' and, handing it back, smiled. I knew what she knew, that for her begging was a business, but I too was a human being.

(45)

A tired old black man sat slumped against the wall round the corner from where I usually stood on Platform 6 to make announcements. I avoided walking near him as he was easily spooked and I wanted him to stay where he was, as it was raining outside. I could see he was genuinely in need. He had placed the regulation Styrofoam cup next to where he was seated, but was silent and did nothing to attract attention either to himself or the cup. I speculated that the coins passers-by might drop in the cup were his only source of income. The travellers and other professional beggars were responsible for making his life that much harder. I watched the way they abandoned small change, only bothering to keep silver and pound coins. Whenever I could I gathered up these coppers and transferred them to a real beggar when no one was looking.

(46)

I was singing the third part in a three-part harmony rendition of 'A Hard Day's Night' with two Swiss buskers at the foot of escalators 9 and 10. We achieved an authentic Beatles sound and were rewarded with smiles from the passing public. Something suggested it was time to move on and just as I had turned the corner a British Transport Police Sergeant pounced on the Swiss duo and told them they could be arrested for singing and playing their guitar. After they had gone the policeman came up to me and told me not to worry, he had moved the buskers on. Had, he said, put the fear of God into them. I wondered what he would have made of my participation had he arrived a minute earlier, made my excuses and walked away feeling downcast at the lack of permitted joy.

(47)

We were issued with two pairs of Doctor Martens black air-soled shoes as part of our uniform. The box said they were the most comfortable shoes in the world. I already owned a second-hand brown pair I wore all the time and they were great. Were the uniform issue shoes subtly different? They looked like normal Doc Martens, except for the small Underground logo tag stitched into the uppers for tax reasons. The leather was a little stiff, but wasn't that always the case for new shoes? They simply had to be broken in and polished into a more pliable state, like people.

During the weekend I wore them around my flat, hoping to accustom my feet to the stiff shoes. I polished them three times. I stuffed them with newspaper. And for a few days they seemed OK. But then it began.

The shoes hurt me and I realised I had been taught something rather strange in Japan: always to ignore minor pain and discomfort. So I did. Consciously I walked without limping, although I knew a buried part of my mind was calculating how long it would be until I got home and could take off the accursed shoes. After five or six days of suffering, my toes began to bleed. I ignored the fact that my socks were caked with blood when I took off my shoes in the early afternoon. It was a battle of wills. I will not surrender to a pair of shoes! I told myself. I would wait them out. They would eventually soften, wouldn't they? Isn't that what shoes always did?

The shoes were unchanged after three weeks. I noticed that every fifth or sixth step I had to limp. I fought to correct this, increasing the pain significantly. Ordinary tasks became extraordinarily difficult. I no longer moved about confidently. Anyone watching me for a minute or two would notice I was wounded. Were I a gnu and they a cheetah, I would be moving up the order of likely prey.

I had tried everything. The shoes were the right size. I had worked on them with saddle soap and with polish. I had acquired shoe trees. I left them in warm places, propitiated them so that they would be reasonable and desist in their torture. I was for ever washing bloody socks. My toes resembled the toes of a trench war veteran, or a POW forced to march huge distances. If I continued, there seemed to be a real chance of inflicting permanent damage to my feet. I would have to admit defeat. Only then did I observe what my colleagues were wearing: hardly anyone had on the regulation issue shoes.

(48)

He is a barbarian, and thinks that the customs
of his tribe and island are the laws of nature.

G. B. SHAW

Having to wear a uniform takes away our freedom
to dress as we feel. But how free are we anyway? Is
clothing a form of expression? Or one of the ways by
which we declare our conscious or unconscious membership of a tribe? Or both? Goths. Suits. Smart-casual.
Counter-culturalists. Non-conformists keen to conform
to a visible display of their presumed non-conformity.
Jalaluddin Rumi, the thirteenth-century mystic and
poet, said that apparently opposed things are often co-
operating on another level. Clothing is an example of
this phenomenon.

(49)

Standing in the shade, under the awning of a bar, in
the main street of Arusha, Tanzania, just standing,
enjoying the relative cool of the shadow. A group of
soldiers walk down the street, looking in my direction.
I am wearing army surplus fatigues and, taking me for
an officer, they salute as they pass. I return the salute,
as I would a smile, a greeting or a wave.

Asmara, Eritrea, leaning against a wall. In the distance a soldier shouts and gestures at me. For emphasis
he levels his AK47 and immediately fires several bursts.
The bullets slam into the wall above my head. They
make a curious pinging noise as they ricochet, which I
hear clearly as shock kicks in: I am a target! And I realise

the uniform I am wearing is a mistake and that I might be killed because of it.

I am watching television. Watching men in white coats. Experts. They explain that the newly discovered ingredient XDF has once again further potentiated their particular brand of toothpaste and that only fools will resist rushing out to buy some, this very minute.

I hide behind my Underground uniform each day, the real me nearly completely concealed. I feel like a birdwatcher, a twitcher, successfully camouflaged, watching and recording. The quarry has no idea what is happening – and would not have cared had it known.

(50)

The boots I replaced the torturous shoes with had been with me to France and back, unworn. I bought them in a charity shop in Sussex on the way to a ferry crossing. They were workmen's leather boots with a steel toecap and padded ankles and were slightly too large. It took a while for me to recognise that they had a different and quite distinct disadvantage; the soles were unyielding and worn day after day they made my feet tired and bruised.

This may not seem like a big deal until you remember the bastinado. Beating the feet is painful and disrupts the general health of the victim. Reflexologists believe the whole health of a person can be diagnosed and corrected by feeling and massaging the feet.

(51)

Mental balance is impossible in the absence of physical balance. Rumi said every thought has a physical mani-festation. But the opposite is also true, the body can and does create mental states. Just try limping or walking stooped for a while – or remember what it is like to have a back injury – and see what this does to your overall self-image. Feelings of vitality are reinforced by strong physical associations. How you sit, stand and move are of the utmost significance.

(52)

We were allowed to ascend to street level every so often for 'a blow', a term I had never heard before and came to understand as meaning something between a break and an opportunity to have a smoke. Perhaps, having a 'suck and blow', a more accurate description of smoking, sounded too ridiculous. I do not smoke cigarettes and couldn't find time for the cigars I preferred; in any event, I was not addicted to smoking and didn't crave tobacco for the four hours I worked each morning. For me, a blow meant standing around and breathing the surface air; watching the passers-by whose moods differed from those of their subterranean selves; or sipping a cup of coffee bought from the Bagel Express or Cafe Fred in Argyle Street.

Staring into my Styrofoam cup, and indeed blowing on the hot coffee to render it drinkable, I noticed that a woman was grubbing about a short distance from my feet, but at first I didn't see what she was doing. I looked up to see a middle-aged woman wearing a winter coat and a headscarf, with a cigarette perched between her lips. She looked like an extra from *EastEnders* who would not turn a head in Albert Square, and she was not a dosser, unless she was new to it and had yet to acquire the degree of grime more time would render inevitable.

She had sucked the ash of her cigarette to an inch and a half and it tilted, threatening to fall as she moved around in short bird-like hops, from one nub-end to the next. She was collecting smokes. I watched her pick up a fairly long discarded cigarette and roll it between her stubby fingers to restore the flattened tube to a rounder, more cigarette-like shape. Then she put it in her pocket and hopped off, eyes fixed keenly on the pavement searching for treasure. Was this hunting or gathering? I imagined her ancestors doing precisely the same thing and with the same intensity and concentration perhaps 10,000 years ago, but gathering berries or grubs instead of nub-ends.

(53)

A tale, fictitious or otherwise, illuminates truth.
JALALUDDIN RUMI

We moved towards the light, keeping close to the wall and running in short bursts of energy. I was white, my grandfather a dappled grey, and despite the filth it was a family tradition to pride ourselves on our standards of personal grooming. 'Stop,' said grandfather and I halted at once. Doing what you were told at once was, I knew, sometimes the difference between life and death in the tunnels. The sectioned oval of light revealed a concrete platform and there were people standing and staring into space; they had vacant unalert looks on their faces, a waking sleep, so different from us, our eyes only rested in real sleep. I doubted if they would recognise danger until it was too late or could move quickly when it came. I had no idea how they found food or a mate in this strangely sluggish state. I was genuinely puzzled and wanted to ask grandfather about it all.

'Grandfather,' I whispered, 'may I ask a question?' He squeaked his assent. 'What are they doing?' 'That, my child,' he began, 'is what we call the human race. A contemptible condition. They move around without purpose at great speed. They always seem unhappy and project a feeling of hostility and tension. Sometimes they are drunk or drugged. Always silent when alone or in groups they do not seem connected to. No sense of our standards of community and hospitality. Best to leave close proximity to the Metro mice; we rats prefer the tunnels as far from the human race as we can manage.'

A small child is standing a little way from its mother, looking curiously into the tunnel. As a train approaches, its headlights reflect a thousand staring eyes twenty or thirty yards into the tunnel. The child begins to giggle, to jump up and down, but no one else sees what he sees or can guess what he is laughing at.

(54)

Opposite where I am standing gratefully filling my lungs, there is a youngster sitting in a doorway. He has a couple of days' growth of adolescent beard, the ubiquitous hooded sweatshirt, hood pulled up. His knees are covered with a blanket and propped next to him is an improvised sign, black marker pen on corrugated cardboard torn from a box which used to contain Walker's crisps. The sign says 'Hungry and Homeless – Please Help'. As mostly tourists wander down Argyle Street, perhaps in search of Liberty's and the Palladium, it's a good pitch; he calls to anyone who comes within range. Predictably he is asking for 'spare change'.

I watch him for a few minutes. His expression is fixed, but not the vacant gaze of the smackhead, just unchanging as if he has no involvement in what is going on around him, is able to function on autopilot and has nothing invested in the success or failure of his pleas. There and then I couldn't find any answers to the dozen questions which buzzed around my brain and so turned to descend the steps into Oxo when a familiar noise caught my attention and made me look back across the street. The sound, an irritating regular bleeping sequence, seemed to be coming from beneath the homeless youth's blanket. He confirmed this by reaching out a mobile phone and talking into it. I stared, but he didn't see me or meet my eyes and after a few seconds his blank look dissolved into a dazzling smile. It's good to talk, I thought, and smiled a small reflected smile of my own.

(55)

The chocolate machines found throughout the Underground are owned and managed by a commercial company. There is a freephone number to call in the event of a complaint, but hardly anyone who experiences a problem reads the notice which explains that London Underground are not responsible and can't do anything to help the disappointed chocoholic. Sometimes the disfunctioning machines are simply broken or empty. Sometimes they have been sabotaged.

Once I found a small boy crying next to a chocolate machine and understood at once what had happened. I knew the machine wasn't working and that telling him to phone a freephone number was useless. I led him by the hand to another, working machine and bought him the Wispa bar he had tried to buy for himself. He walked away eating the chocolate and without thanking me, assuming quite naturally that I was simply making the system do what it was meant to do.

Sabotaged machines were often blocked with small pieces of card in the coin return window, so that change and refunded coins would be prevented from falling out until the card was removed. Most chocolate shoppers were in a hurry and they would jump on a train and abandon their change. Over a whole day the coins which failed to fall out would mount up to a significant sum. One of my colleagues pointed out that this was being done and took a Supervisor round to show him how most of the chocolate machines had been tampered with in this way. As a reward he was assigned the duty of checking the machines every day and from time to time he would hand in several pounds in small change he claimed he had found stuck in the blocked machines.

What he failed to explain was that he was responsible for blocking the machines in the first place. That he harvested them each day and was supplementing his salary in tax-free loot from the hurrying hungry public. Although I knew his secret and disapproved of this petty larceny, I was obliged to maintain the code of *omertà* which bound SAs to each other, rendering the idea of finking to the management quite out of the question.

(56)

I could smell kerosene. Four bleak Japanese winters in unheated wooden apartments warmed solely by kerosene stoves made it a familiar scent. I followed the trail to Platform 4 and as I stepped on to the platform could hardly believe my eyes. A young man with a ponytail in a *shalwar khamis* and no shoes was entertaining a small group of tourists. He was a juggler. That he was juggling four clubs was, I suppose, not particularly strange. The unusual thing was that the clubs were on fire.

I had seen flaming clubs juggled like this in public squares all over the world, but never under ground. He saw me, caught his clubs one by one, extinguished them all simultaneously in a bucket of water he had placed nearby and then, snatching up the bucket, he began to run.

(57)

A loud regular thumping noise. I moved towards it and saw at the other end of the platform a teenage boy bouncing a basketball. He was trying to rebound the ball off the ceiling of the tunnel, but could not make the ball bounce high enough. The limit of the elasticity of the ball, or some combination with the boy's strength, was about eighteen feet.

(58)

Three boys, two white one black, skated past me at speed. One of them, inches from the edge of the platform, was wearing a Walkman and could not hear when I yelled at them to stop. Even the ones who could hear ignored me and they all turned into a cross passageway skating on to the parallel platform. By the time I caught up they were sheepishly removing their skates and gingerly tiptoeing on to a halted train. The driver waved to me. 'I told 'em I'm not moving until they've taken those bleedin' skates off. Bloody kids!'

(59)

My friend Graham told me about his adventures in Baja California. He wrote a book about the time he spent walking, exploring and living in the desert, and after months alone there returned to his job as a teacher at an inner-city school. He told me how he had tried to inspire a class of sixteen-year-olds into imagining the possibilities of adventure and escape. 'But, sir,' they'd all chorused, 'we've got no money. You need money to travel.' He told them he hadn't needed money. That when he arrived in Baja he had just £200 and did odd jobs and lived off the land to keep going. They refused to believe or accept this and the plaint about the insurmountable money barrier was raised again and again. 'They needed more imagination, not money,' said Graham.

(60)

A group of Japanese youths, dressed entirely in black. Some have dyed hair, blond or red. These kids are thought to be 'from another planet' in the Japanese phrase used in the Tokyo media to describe their local-ised delinquency. They fool around near the edge of the platform. I walk over and, using my best gangster voice, yell at them, '*Hora! Abunai yo! Dame da!*' (Hey, it's dangerous, don't do that!) They make noises of surprise and dissent at the talking ape of a foreigner who miracu-lously seems able to speak Japanese. Upping the volume a couple of notches I scream '*Ore wa namero na!*' (Don't fuck with me!) and in a quick lurch slap the nearest boy on the top of his head, like a Japanese school teacher. They flinch collectively, and at once commence the spas-tic nodding bows of the cowed young and retreat to the platform wall. I feel like a conjuror who has just succeeded in making a rabbit disappear.

(61)

Riding the subway in no hurry. Early for the class I am to teach that morning and able to take my time. Sud-denly the train alarm sounds. There is a commotion on the platform. Staff run up and down shouting something I cannot understand. There are police too – but not ordinary cops. They are in kevlar body armour and I know they are *kidotai*, Tokyo's riot police. The man next to me says there has been a gas attack and we must leave the station at once.

Many passengers cover their mouths with their hand-kerchiefs, although I cannot smell anything strange. 'Don't run. Don't run. Please exit the station at once.' At the surface there was a kind of chaos. I heard the words for 'death' and 'terrorist' without being able to piece the story together.

We listen to the radio at the language school and

learn that Aum Divine Truth, a cult, have attacked the subway with Sarin nerve gas. Twelve are dead and thousands injured. Looking at a subway map I count the two stations separating me from directly experiencing nerve gas, as I sip my tea and nibble on a digestive biscuit.

(62)

Most days I remained on platform level for my entire four-hour shift. I didn't need to go to the lavatory. I didn't see the point in a cup of tea, began to see the struggle with boredom as a challenge to self-discipline and countered it with exercises in heightening each sense in turn: first careful observation; then listening closely; finally sniffing the air like an animal. Only the senses of touch and taste were redundant, except perhaps that the way I walked and stood and moved my arms, usually carrying an extension mike and radio, were also mindful and deliberate.

Apart from boredom I also had to cope with the reactions of colleagues to my stoicism. I gradually learned that my long periods on the platforms were thought to be setting a bad precedent and I was often asked if I wouldn't like a break or a cup of tea. It took a while before I realised that this 'concern' was designed to cause me to fall into line with established platform duties behaviour. This included arriving on the platform at least fifteen minutes after starting work; having at least one PNR and at about 9.30 ascending to street level for a blow or a cup of tea. I lightly brushed off these suggestions without making anything of what I was doing. I just said I wasn't thirsty; didn't need to go to the lavatory; wasn't bored. Once I had been classified as eccentric rather than engaged on showing anyone up, I was left alone.

(63)

I arrived one morning to discover that my duties had been changed: for the first two and a half hours I was to work at ground level on the Argyle Street exit barrier and then to resume my northbound platform patrols. I had acquired a conservative approach to new tasks and could easily understand why this was normal in blue-collar occupations. I suppose I was simply nervous about doing something I might mess up. The exit barrier experience was as far from that of Platform 6 as possible. Although during the rush-hour downstairs there were large numbers of people being disgorged from trains, they were mostly unlikely to acknowledge me in any way. A few might ask a question, most just walked past as quickly as they could. On the barriers a different mind-set operated. The barrier behaviour had a note of desperation about it. Like an escaping prisoner, most passengers wanted to get to the other side of the wire as quickly as possible. A ten-second delay would trigger a chain reaction of anger and frustration.

(64)

Each time I encountered a busker I couldn't help wondering about the official policy: that they were obstructions and the noise they made was a safety risk. The reasoning was poor, claiming that music might drown out an important safety message. This neglected the fact that the stationwide PA was always fading in and out of audibility, and that there were large numbers of permanently 'deaf' Walkman wearers. So many young people chose to lock themselves into a bubble of sound in which they could glide along unaffected by the stresses outside in the transit environment. Their chances of hearing any safety announcements were precisely nil, but this had probably not occurred or did not worry them.

(65)

Music in this strange subterranean place had additional implications. The authorities were behaving in a diametrically opposed fashion in New York: there was an officially sanctioned and sponsored programme allowing buskers to perform in subway stations. Preliminary results said that the public liked it, it cheered them up. What about canned music? In the Newcastle Metro system, a newspaper reported that teenage vandalism had been reduced to incidental levels by a simple method: instead of playing contemporary pop hits over the public address as muzak, they decided to switch to a classical repertoire. The effect was dramatic. The gangs of youths who usually spent a lot of their time hanging out in stations and the tunnels couldn't stand it. They left to find somewhere more to their taste. Delius's symphonic poem, Sea Drift, was spectacularly effective and caused mass migrations instantaneously. The savings in money terms were nearly £500,000 – the average annual cost of repairs to vandalised equipment and public spaces.

(66)

Pete seemed agitated and was in mid-bitch to a Supervisor as I walked into the Operations Room. I made myself a cup of tea and listened with half an ear to what he was saying. Pete had just argued with Pierre, a fractious black busker who liked to pick fights and generally cause trouble – and who, I gathered, was still hanging about in the passageways somewhere in the station. 'After my tea I'm going back down – and if he's still playing I'm really going to tell him this time,' said Pete. I knew Pierre by sight, but had never spoken to him, nor had I witnessed his aggressive behaviour. I had heard him busk and noticed that he sang off-key and strummed a guitar in a barely competent way – neither especially terrible or noteworthy in a good way. Live muzak. Background noise best ignored, which was what I would have done with Pierre the pest. But the rules said we had to move buskers on. And this was doubly so for buskers who had made themselves disliked.

I forgot about this, finished my tea and went to work at the Argyle Street exit. After half an hour there was a sudden urgency in the radio traffic. Something was happening downstairs. Someone had been hit. There was a chase. Several SAs and a Supervisor were involved and I could tell from the snatches of radio chatter it was Pierre they were after. After they had cut off his attempt to leave on a Central Line train a Supervisor radioed to say Pierre was making for the surface and was trying to escape via the Argyle Street exit and that we should stop him. As I took this in Pierre appeared. He held his uncovered guitar by the neck in his left hand and broke into a run as he stepped off the escalator. I quickly slid in front of him and formally asked to see his ticket.

'Leave me the fuck alone! What you want with me, man?' 'Can I see your ticket?' I repeated. I guessed he didn't have one and noticed he was nearing the exit wickets and seemed to be preparing to jump the barrier. So I grabbed his right wrist with my left hand and just held on. He shook his hand and spun round and round desperately trying to shake off my grip. 'What the fuck, man!' I let him move into the exit gate and then stopped and anchored my weight so he couldn't pull me any further.

A number of thoughts flashed quickly but calmly through my head. If he tries to hit me I will stop the blow and then lock and pin him. If he doesn't attack I will simply hold on. When a Supervisor gets here, I'll do whatever I'm told to do. Some SAs had arrived and they were milling around, very loosely surrounding Pierre. Pierre was yelling abuse, offering to fight us all. He still hadn't managed to shake me off and it was not difficult to hold him. His arms were thin. He was slightly built, dreadlocks hanging like cheap curtains around his fox-like angular face, and he was, I guessed, in his early forties. Apart from the remote chance of a knife, he was not a real danger to anyone. At that precise moment I felt sorry for him and didn't want to hurt him.

Pierre leaned forwards, lowering his head and began to bite my hand. The bite was intended to hurt, but I was so detached I hardly registered the fact that his incisor teeth had penetrated the skin of my hand and drawn blood. It didn't hurt. From the way the others were behaving it seemed clear that no concerted effort would be made to arrest Pierre now – and so I decided to let go.

At once Pierre danced through the barrier and turned to deliver a parting tirade. I slowly followed him.

He ran up the exit stairs and, deciding that he was now on neutral ground, shouted at me that we should fight then and there. I smiled and in my iciest voice replied, 'Later.' And, after a pause, 'Have a nice day,' as he disappeared into the Oxford Street crowds.

The bite might be serious. Human bites were said to carry a far greater risk of a variety of unpleasant infections than dog bites or many other types of animal attack. I was given an antiseptic swab and told to go to University College Hospital immediately. At the hospital the doctor made a drawing of the wound, dressed it and gave me a prescription for antibiotics. He said the antibiotics were prophylactic – and as I take medicine only when seriously ill I decided to wait and see if an infection developed. Only then would I take the antibiotics, but not otherwise.

The wound did not become inflamed or show other symptoms of being infected. But what of invisible infection? On the internet I found a case of an eighty-two-year-old man in Florida who had contracted HIV when bitten by a drug-using prostitute whose car had broken down and where he had stopped to help change a tyre. There was also the risk of hepatitis, syphilis and even human necrotising bacterium – the dreaded flesh-eating infection which consumes you alive from within. There was a staff consensus that assaults earned you a paid holiday and although I was fine and wanted to go back to work, I knew that my keenness would be unpopular and considered to set a negative precedent. I took three days off to recover from the nervous shock of the possibility that I was now being eaten alive by an unstoppable superbug.

(67)

Chatting with a Bakerloo driver on Platform 4 I swiftly snatched off my uniform cap and whacked him with it on the bare arm he had stuck out of the window of his driver's cab. 'What the . . . ?' he said, taken aback. 'Mosquito,' I replied, pointing to the squashed remains on his arm. I had noticed them the day before yesterday and had been struggling to get a closer look to see what we might be up against before making a report. Armed with an empty Volvic water bottle I coaxed a colleague to stand at the headwall of Platform 4, sleeves rolled up, to act as bait in my insect hunt. 'Try to look tasty,' I said. 'How the hell do you look tasty to an insect?' he answered, not unreasonably, and from the look on his face I could see he was less than fully committed. I congratulated myself for failing to explain to him that the mosquito is man's deadliest enemy, easily responsible for more deaths than any other creature or human that has ever lived. After a minute or two I could see a couple of mosquitoes buzzing around *The Bait*. 'Don't move. Keep very, very still,' I said, slowing down and slurring my words and taking the lid from the Volvic bottle as I crept forward. The insect was feeding on my friend's arm, just above his elbow. In the silence of the empty platform I imagined I could almost hear the blood being greedily sucked. A single smooth movement from behind and I had positioned the bottle over the fly, it took off, moving further inside the bottle, and I secured the lid. 'Gotcha!'

Two days later I had concluded that my captive was neither *culex* (the vector for elephantiasis) which has bushy antennae and a level body, *anopheles* (which transmits malaria) which leans forward at an acute angle and has distinctive legs, or *aedes* (dengue and yellow fever) which has a level body and black-and-white striped legs, so I arranged to meet an old school friend who was an expert entomologist. I pulled out the Volvic bottle after our cappuccinos had been brought over. 'Where on earth did you get this?' said my friend. 'This species is entirely unknown in England.'

I remembered reading accounts of residents of housing estates situated near Gatwick and Heathrow airports, some of whom had never set foot overseas, contracting malaria. The mosquitoes which gave them the disease had arrived, like everyone else, by jumbo jet; insect stowaways from the malarial tropics. And now I wondered if they had managed to find their way further into our transport infrastructure. Arrive by jet, travel around by Tube, live in the dark, damp tunnels under a blood-filled metropolis.

I went home and dug out my medical kit, the veteran of hundreds of journeys, and liberally doused the shirt sleeves and trouser legs of my Tube uniform in undiluted DEET (diethyltoluamide) and Scandinavian Tundra Oil. It was a killer combination that had kept me safe in jungle and marsh and, like a boy scout, I knew it paid to be prepared.

(68)

There was an emergency on the southbound platforms. Everything was happening at once. I had a stopped train, held in the platform because of a suicide further up the Victoria Line, and now there was another emergency. Listening to the radio traffic I realised someone was having a heart attack on Platform 5. Without waiting to be told I ran up and down my own platform calling into the train for a doctor or nurse to identify themselves. A man carrying a briefcase came up to me and said he was a doctor. I told him we had a heart attack victim and would he please come with me.

We ran down the platform and turned into the bridge passageway, taking the stairs two or three at a time. It was exciting. I felt like an ambulance speeding to a crash site, knowing that even a few seconds might mean the difference between brain damage and a good recovery. I radioed as I ran. 'I have a doctor and we are on our way now,' adding, 'where exactly is the passenger having the heart attack?' It turned out he was now on Platform 3, the southbound Bakerloo platform.

As we arrived I looked at the scene and the doctor took over. Douglas Tate, a first-aid-trained SA, was sitting on the man's chest, frantically giving heart massage alternated with mouth to mouth. The victim, a man in his sixties or seventies, showed no signs of being alive. His clothes were dishevelled, his tie torn down and collar opened by the first aider. He looked drunk, undignified, not responsible. The phrase 'the dignity of death' came unbidden into my mind. I would not wish to die on an Underground platform, I thought. His false teeth lay to one side, like an abandoned prop for a failed joke – the teeth seemed to need something, lying there, a glass of water into which to settle perhaps, to complete the scene. An installation by Damien Hirst: Dead Man and His Teeth.

The doctor had taken over giving the heart massage, and had nothing new to add to the life-saving repertoire already being tried; he checked the man's pulse, looked at his eyes, asked Douglas how long he had been administering the emergency procedures and, on hearing the answer, decided to give up, pronouncing the man dead.

'I'm afraid he's dead,' said the doctor and we were obliged to believe him.

We took the doctor's business card, as he was anxious to leave, had a train to catch at King's Cross, and he walked off in the direction of my platform. I had been keeping the curious back while the doctor worked. A Supervisor said we should move the body off the platform into a cross passageway, and so two SAs picked the man up by his arms and legs. The elderly corpse was not heavy and didn't seem dead now that he was, more like someone just taking a nap. I bent down and picked up the discarded false teeth, putting them in my pocket – they were a trip hazard lying there.

Just as the body was placed gently on the ground in the passageway, the paramedics arrived. We told them a doctor had pronounced the man dead. 'Yeah, what do doctors know?!' said the first paramedic as he opened his kit and began work at a furious pace. Unlike the doctor, they were well tooled up, carrying bags full of potions and strange implements. They injected something, was it adrenaline?, directly into the man's chest and then began to set up a defibrillator. TV hospital soaps like *ER* had taught me what was going to happen next, but the context seemed bizarre – not an emergency room, but a corridor I walk down every morning.

We formed a physical barrier so the curious could not get in the way or walk where the paramedics were working. Surreally, as they were about to electrocute the dead man, calling out to each other the level of charge and, dramatically but predictably, 'Clear!', someone walked up to me and asked, not what was going on or about the dead man, but a run-of-the-mill everyday normal question: 'Can you tell me the way to the Central Line, please?' As I pointed out how to get there, I heard a pop as the current discharged into the body and out of the corner of my eye saw its effects, the body convulsing. The customer seeking the Central Line did not appear to notice this or indeed anything except me; had she developed tunnel vision, I wondered, watching her as she simply turned and went on her way.

The paramedics had performed a miracle, obtaining a steady pulse, had stabilised his vital signs and were strapping the man, whom I now thought of as Mr Lazarus, never learning his real name, into a stretcher. I had just witnessed someone being brought back from the dead. It was not yet ten o'clock in the morning.

(69)

The genuine smile, a gift, life-affirming, quite unexpected. Why does this feel so affecting? On a train at Brixton a man comes along mumbling and, caught out in the embarrassment of talking to himself, suddenly smiles at me, which I return. A young boy getting on a train on my platform half turns and flashes a smile at me for no discernible purpose and I feel elated for half an hour. An elderly woman looking around for the route to her connection sees me and the way to go at the same time, she smiles thanks, although I have done nothing, and I beam too to thank her for the smile.

Might it not be some sort of test of civilisation how often we smile at strangers, spontaneously, without fear, and without expecting anything in return? Expecting nothing except for an acknowledging smile to say thanks; thanks for reminding me I am human. When did you last smile in this way and not because you were flirting with someone to whom you were attracted?

(70)

Three aphorisms taken at random from last night's TV, each from a different programme:

Bacchus gives life to wandering men.

Of each particular thing, what is it in itself? – Marcus Aurelius

The same is different every day.

(71)

Standing on the edge of the platform, I wonder if the fact that jumping on to the tracks is possible is the explanation for why suicides occur. Anything possible will eventually happen. Most of us have experienced the urge to throw ourselves off tall buildings. When this happens I move away from the edge. Some move towards it – and a few pass over the edge and jump.

(72)

William James in *Principles of Psychology* explains: The mind is at every stage a theatre of simultaneous possibilities. Consciousness consists in the comparison of these with each other, the selection of some and the suppression of the rest by the reinforcing and inhibiting agency of attention.

(73)

When you have fallen once, tread warily,
So you do not once again lose your footing.
SAADI

Walking along the platform I would usually kick papers and rubbish to the side so no one would slip or trip. It was necessary to keep an eye out for the number one slip hazard and killer of the elderly in supermarkets: the isolated grape. Green grapes were the worst, being harder than black grapes to see. Grapes were frequently left lying where they fell, whereas the clichéd hazard, the banana skin, although more numerous, was usually kicked against a wall or left perched on top of a chocolate machine or Way Out sign. Once I had watched someone slide along Platform 4 as if hitting a patch of black ice in a car, nearly losing their footing. The unfortunate customer had slipped on a small pool of frozen peas, still frozen hard, which I quickly kicked in to the rail well. The customer berated me in odd terms, 'Why d'you allow these peas to be left here, then?' There was certainly no ready answer.

(74)

I see a small piece of paper on the floor and prod it with my boot. It is light blue and silver, the silver reflecting the fluorescent overhead lights, and is almost sparkling as I bend down to look at it. There is white printing and it seems to be a leaflet advertising something. The brightly coloured paper reminds me of the pamphlets which used to fall like confetti out of the legal journals

I had spent most of my early adult life reading. I pick it up: it is advertising a legal textbook published by Sweet & Maxwell. I am shocked to read the co-author's name. An old acquaintance, who was a partner in a City firm of solicitors when we knew each other, has now become a barrister and Professor of Law. The last time I read his name in print was when it appeared next to mine in a notice of a lecture we would give at Oxford University. Now he was a full professor and I was removing the small handbill advertising his most recent book from the middle of an Underground platform so that no one would step on it awkwardly and fall over.

The handbill was three things all at once, occupied three dimensions. It advertised a book, had been lost or discarded and was now, given its precise position, a safety hazard. For me it was also a symbol of a past life and my teacher of how something may be many things if perceived in the right way.

(75)

I turn on to the eastbound platform and see Salman Qureshi wrestling with a man in the suicide pit down on the tracks. I run up, ready to jump down and mix it, but wondering why a fight should have migrated to such a dangerous place. Had they struggled and fallen down?

As I draw up alongside, things become clear. Salman has a hand on the man's sleeve, but the man is obviously having an epileptic fit, not fighting as I first thought. Wong Tsu, an SA, is at the other end of the platform, having used the tunnel telephone to turn off the traction current. Tony Aristides, another SA, is also there and I feel superfluous. Salman tells me to ring the Line Controller to update him on what is happening, that we are trying to move the man off the tracks and will tell him as soon as we have done this. I run to the autophone and call the emergency number; the number I need is printed on a card stuck to the wall. After doing what I have been told I run off down the adjacent platform calling for anyone with medical training. Why I am always able instantly to find a doctor I have no idea, but like a genie a beautiful woman tells me in the accents of Ingrid Bergman she is a doctor, Swedish, but working in London.

We run round the corner and bravely the doctor, holding her skirt with one hand, immediately clambers down on the tracks to talk to the man. He is no longer in convulsions, seems not to know where he is. I begin to suspect he can't understand English, but even if he could, it would have been difficult to follow what the Swedish doctor is saying because of her heavy accent. Even as pure sound, the steady harmonies of the melodious rising-then-falling noises which emerge from her beautiful lips – 'Koom oon nooo, youdel doon woont too geet hoort nooo' – would soothe anyone. He calms down and responds to being led on to the platform by the doctor's manicured fingers and Salman's less appealing oily hands.

(76)

Salvatore was Italian and could understand only a little English. We managed by signing and gentle force to move him away from the trains and upstairs to the Operations Room. The Swedish lady doctor had confirmed he was having an epileptic seizure, an absence she called it, and doubted if Salvatore would recollect how he came to be standing on the rails of the Central Line during rush-hour. Salman, who had done everything exactly right, ably assisted by Wong and Tony, was only in the right place at the right time because of an earlier disruption causing delays on the Central Line. This delay probably saved Salvatore's life; but I reluctantly recognised it was not something I could make use of when next being berated for the failing service.

(77)

A young woman complains that the Asian boy who sits inside the tiny newsagent's vending booth in the Bullring, from whom she had just purchased a packet of mints, had been masturbating and that his hand was sticky when he handed over her change. John, a Supervisor, asks if she wishes to involve the police, if she is willing to wait to make a statement and she says yes. He then stalks off to spy on the boy for visible signs of arousal.

'He was wiping his hand with a tissue as I walked past,' said John, when he returned a few minutes later, 'the dirty bugger.' This was taken as damning evidence. In the minds of most males, tissues and masturbation are as connected as ham and eggs.

When the British Transport Police officers arrive, the boy, only seventeen I learn later, is told to close his stall and is led away to the Police Room for questioning. The woman's statement claimed she had seen his hand moving in the rhythmic manner so characteristic of the onanist, she had also 'remembered' that he had a lusty look on his face and may have moaned as he handed over her packet of Polos. And that sticky hand wouldn't go away; it was the final nail in his coffin – referred to both by her in her statement and confirmed by the Supervisor who had witnessed the suspicious hand-wiping.

The boy is questioned for nearly three hours. I cannot imagine what is being asked, but expect the same questions are being put to him again and again. His employer is summoned. The boy finally confesses. He is formally cautioned by the BTP, then sacked by his employer. No one I ask seems to know his name.

Although masturbating in a barely concealed place during the morning rush-hour in the second busiest Underground station in London is a vulgar, hazardous and stupid thing to do, I feel sorry for the boy. And hostile towards the woman with her horror of sticky change and whose complaint cost a stranger his job. Seventeen-year-olds masturbate when they are bored. Selling newspapers and sweets is boring. Thankfully they are traditionally secretive about it – and it's only because of this that you don't see them at it everywhere you look.

(78)

I stand at the bottom of escalators 1, 2 and 3, all of which lead to the Argyle Street exits. It is an intersection which, in addition to the escalators, has five passages leading to the three lines that merge at Oxford Circus. As there are eight 'legs' which join the small circular area, it is known by station staff as the Spider. One morning I saw a small brown object lying on the ground in the middle of the Spider and I stooped and picked it up. It was a rubber spider, designed to resemble a tarantula or bird-eating spider, with long legs and rubber nodules as 'hairs' on the legs, the kind of spider that comes threaded with a piece of elastic so you can bounce it up and down.

I made enquiries, but no one had lost the spider, nor did it seem to be a practical joke. No one knew anything about it. I took it to the Operations Room and it was adopted as a mascot. For the few days before it disappeared never to return, it bounced happily in the glass enquiry window.

The Spider is a good place to watch the flow of people; it always made me think of Heraclitus: *You can never step twice into the same river*. In the rush-hour hardly anyone approaches with a question. Not until the tourist phase, which generally starts at about ten o'clock, is this a place where you need to do any work.

Every day a woman passes this way and if I am there I wait for her. She is unremarkable, except for her 'dog'. It has reddish fur, seems well behaved and trots along on its lead without any trouble at all. When they reach the base of the escalator she drops the lead and nods, holding out her arms, and the 'dog' jumps into them. 'Dog' and woman step on to the escalator and ascend together, sandwiched neatly between two others.

Once when she hesitates, frisking her pockets for her Travelcard, I ask her, 'What kind of dog is that? He's clever,' and she replies, 'It's not a "he" it's a "she,"'' and, 'It's not a dog, it's a vixen.' The odd dog is a tame fox.

Another woman has what at first I take to be the ugliest baby I have ever seen, although I just caught a glance as she hurried past. The next day I position myself to intercept her and confirm that the diabolical infant is not an hallucination. I realise at once it is a baby chimp in a pale blue cardigan, matching woolly hat and a nappy. On an impulse I asked her what kind of nappies she uses. 'Huggies for Boys', she calls over her shoulder as she is carried away in a tide of higher primates seeking ascendancy.

(79)

My friend Wong Tsu is the son of immigrant parents. He was brought up speaking both Chinese and English and speaks English with a London accent. He has a boyish, friendly face and a schoolboy's unruly hair, which always seems to need combing, especially when he removes his hat. I admired his devotion to his parents very much: he was in the process of buying a house in which they would all live together and I don't suppose it would have occurred to him to think of this course of action as any kind of sacrifice; it was simply the natural thing to do. Before working on the Underground he had done various jobs, but I never pressed him for details until one day he told me about working in a Chinese restaurant. He had been a Dim Sum chef. 'Why did you quit?' I asked. 'It was very difficult. Always too hot – and the pay was no good.' 'Well, if it's too hot in the kitchen ... but the important point is can you make Char Siu Cheung Fun?' I said. His face lit up, 'You know about Cheung Fun?' 'Of course, I spent most of my teenage years in and out of Chinese restaurants with my Kung Fu teacher.'

(80)

So as we field the busy and the angry, the ticketless and the lost, for an hour or so neither Wong nor I is paying attention. We are lost to the here and now, in another place. We are cooking. I get him to shout the details step by step to teach me how to make Char Siu Cheung Fun. For those unacquainted with this strangely addictive dish, it translates as Five Spiced Pork in Rice Flour Rolls and is a Cantonese speciality served as Dim Sum, or Heart's Ease, small steamed snacks eaten for breakfast and lunch.

(81)

Wong Tsu had developed the habit of arriving precisely eight minutes late for work and was having difficulties with one or two Supervisors who had decided to lean on him. I asked him why he was late so precisely and wondered if he couldn't simply catch the bus before the one he currently caught. But he just shrugged and I knew the reason was he didn't enjoy the job as much as he had done before starting on the pattern of late arrivals. He was an example of how to ruin good material. He had arrived keen and friendly and helpful and had been exposed to those who played the system for all it was worth and got away with it so often that it was hard to conclude that they were wrong and not to be copied. Additionally, this job had no visible means for feeding back praise; if you didn't talk much to the Supervisors then it was impossible to develop a relation-ship with them – and anyway Wong was just too young to do this.

(82)

It's very early in the morning and I'm in a café. On the table in front of me is a cooked breakfast, what's still called a traditional English breakfast, even though hardly anyone has the time to eat it these days, other than at weekends or when on holiday. Across the room a workman in clothes marked with paint stares into *The Sun*, drinks his tea and draws deeply on a cigarette. I am a smoker, yet the idea of smoking first thing in the morning revolts me. For me it is a leisure activity, a restful thing and who needs to rest the moment after they have woken from sleep? Out through the glass window an elderly man walks past. In his hand is an open can of Tennent's Extra. He drinks it and walks on. I am a drinker, yet the sight of this man depresses me and I realise that had I seen the same man with the same dosser's preferred hooch twelve hours later I would have felt differently.

(83)

I liked to walk around the station looking at the advertising posters. When I noticed a new one I would sometimes not read it, saving it for a particularly powerful attack of under-stimulation. Whenever I did this I remembered the story of the shipwrecked man who saved reading the label of a can of beans for what he took to be his birthday (or was it Christmas Day?), having nothing else to read and anticipating the treat for weeks in advance.

Sometimes in a more cynical mood I would play the Truth Game. This was simply to look at some advertising and assess instantly if it was largely true or largely a lie. Wandering along the platform muttering, 'lie; lie; lie; half true . . .' I must have been an odd sight. This game had spilled over into my home life, so that whenever an advert for mobile phones or double-glazing interrupted the music on the radio, or the commercial breaks interrupted a TV programme, they received the same treatment. But at home I would shout, '*Lie, damn you!!*'

(84)

Are we, as a society, newly addicted to a culture of the false or has this always been the case? Advertising standards exist to protect the public against false claims, but how effective is this? Field psychologists point out that the mind makes judgements based on associations, so it is an easy matter to deceive it. Just associate something desirable with your product and you create the false idea that by acquiring the product the object or situation desired will follow in its wake. Drink this soft drink and you will have an energetic fun-filled frolic in the sea with a beautiful woman. Use this skin cream and you will halt the march of time and rise to the top of your chosen profession. We can all see this association technique at work, but the problem is that it appeals not to our reason but to our sense of things rooted in another reality. It works at the emotional level, at the level of the childish self, over which reason has been layered like the rings of an onion.

(85)

An advertisement has been posted up for waiting passengers to read, visible on the far wall of the trackside platform area. I walk along the platform for a clearer view. It shows a man supine on a low wall. It is a nice day, perhaps summer, and he has taken off the jacket of his suit and rolled up his shirt sleeves. He has loosened his tie. You can see a briefcase propped against the wall. He is a businessman you think, or, because the wall seems to be part of a campus (it looks like Bloomsbury, is it the University of London? Harvard?), could he be a postgraduate student or a lecturer, even a clever young professor? He is wearing glasses, is handsome, has his eyes closed. From the light and the angle of the shadows we may suppose it is midday and that he has eaten, possibly a sandwich acquired nearby, and is now taking a nap before the onset of a busy afternoon.

Carved into the wall is part of a slogan, but we can read only the word 'Freedom'. This man, the poster is announcing, is somehow free. At least he is free enough to take a nap on a wall in the city on a nice day, albeit in a suit and carrying a briefcase. Is he free from the fear that his briefcase may be stolen while he sleeps? That he may oversleep and miss an appointment in the afternoon on which his immediate future hinges? We cannot tell.

There is a huge bottle of Volvic mineral water incorporated in the side bar of the poster. We are asked to believe that there is a causal connection between drinking bottled water, freedom, summer, the pleasure of a nap, being handsome, having nice clothes and accessories, not fearing theft or worrying about the obligations of the day. Not directly, of course, but by associative thinking. And so, should we not unnaturally desire all these things for ourselves, what could be simpler than to buy Volvic and drink it.

(86)

Another day, another wall. This is what it said:

> Once we were all free. Our home was the forest, the mountain and the ocean.
>
> Then something happened.
>
> We became indoor people. Pen pushers, TV watchers, party animals.
>
> But our souls are still out there.

'Wow!' I thought, 'this must be for me.' I read on, found the answer in the next line:

> GORE-TEX® fabric has the power to transform your life and return you to nature.

PART III

Imbrications

Imbricate – arrange (leaves, the scales of fish etc.), or be arranged, so as to overlap like roof tiles

CONCISE OXFORD DICTIONARY (9TH EDITION)

(1)

I'd been thinking about my life underground, and concluded I was becoming pessimistic. England is a pessimistic culture, but there are some environments where the cynicism and glumness seem to concentrate. The morale of my fellow Tube workers was very low indeed and I felt I was finally succumbing to this. It is not possible to resist negative atmospheres for ever, or even for very long. And so was it now time to move on, time to do something else?

In working at this job I had attempted several things at once. Most things we do day to day possess multi-dimensional aspects, but we do not often 'unwrap' them, as it were, to see the different sides and consider how they interact. So for me, at the practical level, it was a part-time job. Even the phrase 'part-time job' is significant. Whereas I believe all activities which are not play may be said to be work, most of my work was not of a commercial kind. I am not a farmer able to provide a livelihood by my own labours and so I must have a minimum income from somewhere. It gave me the small amount of money I needed in exchange for four hours a day. Significantly, I had time and energy remaining for other things.

(2)

On another level I was experimenting with myself. It was an exercise in low stimulation/low-challenge activity; a means to wean part of my mind from a compulsion for the novel and the dramatic. Or so I thought at first. In fact, most days yielded a share of the surprises and drama of the ordinary. I was acquiring a connoisseur's perspective, closely focused on something limited, in my case the mundanities of an ordinary existence.

(3)

I was working on what philosophers call a big idea: *Is urban man trapped and incapable of realising this?* This question related to a wider consideration of freedom and the doubtful concept of free will in contemporary societies. I was looking at the assumptions we make about our lives. Not to sneer or feel personally superior, but to understand. And thinking is a preparation for living, not a substitute for it. So I needed both the orientation and the experiences.

(4)

It was also honest work. If someone asked me how to get somewhere and I knew, or could find out, then I could genuinely help them. Many kinds of commercial activity rest on degrees of dishonesty. On salesmanship of some kind. On the exercise of power and persuasion that the goods or services being offered are both necessary and useful, when this is often highly disputable. In Japanese feudalism the merchant ranked below the artisan for this reason. We, however, have elevated style over content to an extraordinary degree. Our cultural icons provide no role models and in many cases are fine examples of how not to behave.

(5)

How might a would-be honest man earn his living? is a question which concerned me greatly. A starting point in considering this dilemma seemed to be the question of self-deception: I know this is a lousy lawn-mower I am selling, but at least it cuts the grass. Isn't that enough? *Caveat emptor*. Is this attitude preferable to being unable to see what you are in fact doing? It seemed useful to pan back a bit: no one sets out to be a lawn-mower salesman or a chiropodist however necessary or useful these activities are in themselves. It's the boiling frog.

The boiling frog was a favourite object lesson and it was always hopping into my mind. In order to push back the boundaries of scientific discovery, scientists found out that frogs have nervous systems poorly adapted to register slow incremental change – the technical term is *poikilothermic*. So if you sit one in a saucepan of water and slowly heat it, the poor frog will stay where it is and boil to death.

We become chiropodists or lawn-mower salesmen by a series of imperceptible 'choices' and by the time we realise what we have done, we're boiled.

(6)

You're not a man, you're a machine.
G. B. SHAW

Only in our case, unlike for the unfortunate frog, the boiling can be avoided. And unless you have painted yourself into a corner of obligations, you are always free to change. Even with obligations you can change, it may just take a little more effort . . . No one intentionally sets out to be unaware of the consequences that their lifestyles have on their capacity to perceive reality, to think and feel as human beings rather than as machines designed for the consumption of carefully manufactured and marketed 'needs'. However, what you spend a lot of time doing will have significant effects on you. Show me what a man spends his time doing and I will show you the man. Selecting work with this in mind seemed like a sound approach.

My decision to work on the Underground was based upon several comforting assumptions. That it was temporary. I had not the slightest intention of working there for the rest of my life. I was a visitor – even a tourist or a kind of spy. That it was no part of my self-image, was not what I did. My other 'work' was so much more significant. Not alternative part-time jobs, but work on myself. That no one would be able to guess what I was doing.

(7)

Cultural commentators are presently writing about the twenty-first century as a time of increasing prosperity, yet a time also of greater stresses and diminishing personal happiness. I have seen an advertisement for an Internet banking service which identifies its target customers as 'money rich, but time poor'. So you can be rich and poor at the same time. You can be smart and stupid at the same time. You can be comfortably settled and anxious to move on, at the same time.

(8)

Do we run on rails or are we free? This, for me, was an obsession. Am I a train? Who decided where the tracks lead? Can I get about under my own locomotion, my own steam?

(9)

Liberty means responsibility. That is why most men dread it.
G. B. SHAW

A comment by a fashion designer on his latest fragrance called 'Freedom'.

> 'The concept of FREEDOM is natural for fragrance as it has come to represent the true essence of individuality and the ability to choose for oneself,' said Tommy Hilfiger. 'A fragrance responds differently on every person, just as freedom has a different meaning to everyone.'

If I point a gun at you and tell you to do something and you do it, at one level you choose to do whatever I am demanding. But at another level you are compelled by threatened violence. Let us say, however, that you are a religious person who is prepared for his own death. Perhaps we may regard the threat of violence in such circumstances as an empty one, so the choice is again a real one. There are many other possibilities – but only by becoming aware of the forces which may be operating in any situation, equivalent to the gun at the head in my example, forces which may be compelling, removing the volitional, can we begin to understand what it means to be free.

(10)

My adventures Underground were an important part of my continuing education. A different kind of study. A real life class.

(11)

We are taught that we are free to make choices. It's the way we are educated. Governments everywhere are dedicated to the idea of education and are busy enforcing their own versions of minimal curricula to maintain social and economic progress. But hand in glove with this there is an unnoticed process whereby diversity and original thought are penalised and denied appropriate outlets. John Stuart Mill writing in *On Liberty* was worried about this in the nineteenth century:

> A general state education is a mere contrivance for mould-ing people to be exactly like one another: and as the mould in which it casts them is that which pleases the predomi-nant power in government . . . in proportion as it is efficient and successful, it establishes a despotism over the mind, leading by natural tendency to one over the body.

Any right-minded person will support the idea of edu-cation. Where I may be obliged to depart from the ortho-doxy of such a position is where governments tend to talk about more education and of a standardised kind (as if it were a quantity); I want less, and of a special flexible variety.

In the United Kingdom education is compulsory for a period of roughly eleven years, and, during this time, is more or less a full-time activity. The yield from all this time and effort and employing the focused talents of many dedicated professionals is, to put it rather mildly, somewhat disappointing. It would be odd, for example, if a child had attended a musical school, such as the Menhuin School, and left unable to play a single instrument. But we do not think it odd that graduates of our general educational institutions face the world knowing little of value to themselves or to anyone else.

(12)

A radical approach to education requires a correct understanding of the problem and also of what has been tried so far. Our compulsory schooling is disguised child care, or the corralling of children to get them safely out of the way, so their parents can function economically. This is the primary purpose, and teaching anything worthwhile is secondary. In achieving its primary purpose it is partially successful – although more and more of the inmates are successfully breaking out or behaving so as to guarantee their own exclusion from the system.

The economics and organisational logistics of prisons are unlikely to be the same as those which might successfully apply to schools. Gaols also tend to be compulsory environments where you serve a term and are eventually released. Real schools throughout human history have been institutions where the candidates genuinely want to study and where they have managed to overcome the difficulties of gaining entry. Entry to a real school is based on the capacity and desire to learn.

(13)

To any charges of elitism I plead guilty: education is an elite moulding activity, but at its most successful it produces servants rather than masters. Those who possess a greater capacity understand that this both fits and obliges them to perform duties for the benefit of those who lack these skills and abilities, rather than for personal gain. Our society is currently orientated to the idea that you study in order to benefit yourself.

(14)

Considering my training on the Underground as an example of industrial training, am I overstating the case if I call it fraudulent?

The Big White Folder they gave me on the first day at Training Centre had a slogan, 'Training to Succeed', printed at the top in large blue letters. But what was success in this context, and what might successful training involve? Their objective was presumably to transmit facts, information about technical subjects of relevance to the job we were to do, useful stuff. Such a transmission, I presumed, assumed that this useful stuff would stay with us and might be retrieved from our memories whenever we needed it. That it resided in our memories at all was, it seemed to me, extremely suspect.

We were tested immediately after studying the topics

to be examined. Although there was often a great deal to remember, the testing was structured to test passive memory, by means of multiple-choice questions. Short-term passive memory is not much good to anyone seriously concerned with transmitting knowledge. Most of the useful stuff would be forgotten after four or five days.

(15)

Learning by examining the theory of something is hardly ever the best approach to new knowledge. Far better is to learn by doing, under the eyes of an expert, and to enhance this by studying theory later to contextualise the practical knowledge you have gained. Languages, for example, are more rapidly acquired when taken in through the ear first, without recourse to written materials or grammar treatises. Additionally, something else should be taught in the foreign language being learned to distract attention away from focusing on a word at a time.

Today most learning is institutionalised and follows the format of studying towards examination. This best suits information-based systems of learning and is unsuited to the acquisition of practical skills. The examination system and memory-burdened learning is a hangover from the monastic procedures of the late Middle Ages, when books were scarce and valuable and where it made good sense to memorise them as a security measure and where knowledge was equated with words of divine provenance. Those with good memories for this sort of thing were promoted, sorted by testing. Rote learning and good recall were all you needed to excel.

(16)

In the fairly recent past, not everything was taught in order to be tested by examination. Craft skills and the trades which involved complex craft-like procedures were not transmitted through this kind of approach, but by the master/apprentice contract.

At Oxford Circus I quickly decided which of the Supervisors had that extra something that denotes complete mastery of an environment. I attached myself to them, watching and imitating them in each task, determined to steal their skills.

This master/apprentice system acknowledged a quasi-mystical something which can only be passed by the institution of discipleship, something not taught but caught, by keeping the company of the very able. It encouraged silent observation and learning through doing the tasks set without questioning what they might be for. Wax on, wax off may have been meaningless at first for the Karate Kid, but we all trusted that Mr Miyagi knew what he was doing.

This method is not an analytical means of learning, but is based on trust and the belief that you are studying with someone who embodies what you wish to become. The materials studied and the man are conjoined and to be taken together: the human element was regarded as a key, not just one of several ways in which information might be stored and retrieved. That this proved effective was not least because it was dynamic, always able to adjust any point of emphasis to balance the individual difficulties of the student. It was a tailor-made process, not an off-the-peg ready-made means to half teach the ignorant and congratulate them for their capacity to cram, regurgitate and forget.

(17)

We have moved so quickly into the details and complexities of our studies that we have forgotten the most fundamental question: *What does it mean to know something?* How can we learn to arrive at such knowledge? If we pass an exam in something can we be taken to know it? Our current approach of universal access to education has led not to the emancipation of learning as might be hoped, but to a generation of the learned ignorant.

(18)

A factor in the exemplar system of study, or master/apprentice model, is that there are not enough teachers of this type to go round. Mass education is an attempt to do what cannot be done: the untalented teaching the unwilling. The results are all about us and perhaps we will be better able to ask the right questions if we first accept – and I have already alluded to this view – that for large numbers the primary purpose of school is to corral children for the benefit of their parents and society as a whole. School as a prison, or an institutional means of exercising authority *in loco parentis* to free the parents to do other things.

(19)

In Japan there is a greater reliance on the master/student institution. It exists and is supported by society at all levels. There, crafts skills are valued as intangible cultural assets and craftsmen and women sometimes esteemed as living national treasures. Ordinary people toil for years to learn to serve tea according to a system of etiquette four hundred years old or to write beautifully and are generally admired for it, not ridiculed – how then, by way of contrast, is, say, handwriting regarded in the West today outside the slim ranks of graphologists and calligraphers?

But might it not be objected that following and imitating a master is slavishness, likely to suppress creativity and cancel out individuality? In Japan this question is addressed by a concept sometimes called 'preserve, break and separate', or from a reading of the characters which make up this sentence (*mamoru, yabureru, hanareru*) – *shu-ha-ri*. It describes the stages of the apprentice system. First to master by precise imitation (*shu*); then to understand why the master acts as he does by testing the limits and by experimenting with the 'rules' (*ha*); and finally to break away and do your own thing, but so that your every expression embodies the very essence of what you have learned, form no longer being required (*ri*).

(20)

Theoretical, word-based, study or representational study using other means of synthesising meaning, such as mathematics, is often guilty of confusing representation and reality – *the container with the content* – and provides no sure means to recognise this shortfall when it might be met with in real life and where it actually matters. Consider this: I see a play in which an actor convincingly plays the role of a surgeon. The drama is so absorbing

I forget it is a play and feel anxious for the patient under the surgeon's knife; yet, the surgeon's knife is a prop without a sharp edge, no real operation is taking place, the patient is not ill and I would rather that this particular surgeon did not operate on me were I suddenly to need the attentions of a physician. Why? Because in this example the boundary between representation and reality can be recrossed at will.

(21)

You only really possess what will survive a shipwreck. Not things. Never things. But rather skills. Education should not be about the accumulation of mere information, but instead should aim to induce a variety of skills and abilities. One such skill, in the broadest sense, would be the capacity to find things out: how to study and conduct research; how to recognise seminal knowledge and differentiate between the good and the second-rate. This would yield any necessary information when and only when it was needed. Skills can be acquired only from those who genuinely possess them and have understood them to the extent of knowing exactly how they came to such an estate. Like a guide they may then lead others along pathways they have themselves travelled.

(22)

Finding things out, while an amusing way of spending time, would as a necessary consequence become more directly related to applied usage. Why do you want to know that, when you cannot possibly use the answer? Such a reasonable objection would, in time, fall away. We would seek to find things out in order to solve a specific problem and not simply for its own sake. By encouraging the capacity to see systems as whole operative units, as well as orders of details, and these two things simultaneously at that, it would become possible to develop a sense of reality, currently buried under ten thousand unrelated points of view.

(23)

Well, all of this involves learning through human contact. But what about self-education? What about books and the internet?

I read a lot. I am in pursuit of an elusive quarry, sensed, inferred, but incapable of easy articulation. I am looking for books which possess a quality for which there are no words in English. There are terms which express this concept in other languages, but I am not sure that they will help us and as they have accrued unwanted associations I shall not use them, as it is worse to confuse than to induce a mild sense of curiosity.

I may be able to hint at what I mean by explaining that if I happened to be reading about, say, plumbing, I would first circle the subject and try to detect if a seminal book existed; one so well regarded as to be qualitatively different from all the others. Often there is such a book. It is these books that I read. There is always more to them than the words on a page. Something else has been transmitted and it is this I want. The subjects are not directly relevant to what I am doing, but are of a bewildering variety.

(24)

Can you read too much? What about reading as a compulsion? There are a number of problems associated with compulsive reading. First, that it is compulsive and any compulsion tends to occupy too large a space in your life, growing to fill any additional space which may become available. This involves an opportunity cost and other activities are needed, must if necessary be imposed, to cut the compulsion to manageable proportions. It must be a controlled addiction.

(25)

A related problem is that it leads to a strong sense that all knowledge comes from or is contained in books. This, of course, is not so – indeed, the knowledge we get from books is, for the most part, *light*. By this term I mean it is easily taken in, but not easily absorbed and retained to transform the reader. It is generally read and then forgotten. This is why there is a school of thought which recommends not wide reading, but deep reading of a limited number of texts, which through re-reading are utterly owned, become the property as it were, of the reader, capable of being called to mind at will. Most revealed religions, those having a sacred book, take this approach. Rote learning of poetry and classical texts is of this nature too.

(26)

Moreover, to read about something, however accurately and fully the experience is described, is not the same as having actually experienced it. It is like trying to understand, say, a tempest by taking a whirlpool bath. Perhaps in a sense it is related to the original experience, but it is incapable of conjuring the multi-dimensional range of responses which always go along with living.

(27)

My work at Oxford Circus made it impossible to read for a period of four hours each morning. It was, of course, an opportunity to think – and each day I would reflect and compose lengthy dialogues in my mind while pacing up and down the platform or slowly ascending or descending escalators.

(28)

Is thinking a skill or do we know how to think as an inborn capacity? There are those like Edward De Bono who have made careers claiming that hardly anyone thinks – and it is not difficult to see what they mean. Life in a city is so fast that in general we fill our minds with so large and so continuous a flow of sensory impressions that there is only time to process it – yes or no, and-gates and or-gates – so that most mental processes are mechanical and unable to benefit from the slow stroll of reflection. There is no time and no space in the mind to do this.

(29)

We need to manufacture a space. A space in the mind to sift for the truth, ever alert for subtleties and gradations of meaning or even fuzziness, the apparent contradiction of opposites being simultaneously true. It is a case of less is more. By pacing and performing work which, once I knew what to do, made few demands on me, I had, I realised, and quite by accident, begun to clear a space for serious reflection. I had begun to springclean a sclerotic mental landscape and rediscover some of what I had imperfectly understood from my past adventures. Like all of us, although we do not all come to this realisation, many of my experiences were undigested and in this sense can be said, nearly, not to have happened at all.

(30)

Being in a hurry is not just a state of motion, but is an attitude of mind. On the Underground almost everyone was in a hurry. To get at important lessons, life must be simplified and slowed down. When you are in a hurry this is not possible.

(31)

So an experience is not simply something which has happened to you. Your state of mind during the experience will determine its lasting value. I use the term 'event' to describe that which happens to us, but has no lasting value. Experiences are events which have been prepared for and which can be digested and understood. Experiences change you. Events wash over you and are easily forgotten. Most of what happens to us each day is in the event category.

(32)

So for those of us who are unprepared, or who do not digest the events of our lives, are there no experiences and do we remain the same? In a real sense the difference between the living and the dead is the capacity to transform consciousness through the experiences of living in an aware state. But you get into hot water if you start accusing the apparently living of being dead! And people grow nervous and can't help wondering if they might discover that they are dead too!

(33)

A lot of people seem to think the internet might be used to transform education, but is this likely? The internet has a number of implications for modern societies and for their governments or would-be rulers. But in the area of education it assumes something which is simply not true: that more information will lead to better learning. Or that more fun, education as a game, will lead to more willing learning. Neither of these assumptions is true. Most schools possess libraries. How many school children have read all the books they contain and are clamouring for more information?

(34)

Is there anything wrong with enjoying yourself while studying? Yes, when the enjoyment takes the place of the learning.

(35)

Isn't this just a manifestation of man's drive to be happy? Many of us would perhaps answer the question 'What do you want out of life?' with an answer referring to achieving happiness. However, happiness as a condition is meaningful only as a contrastive state. Without unhappiness we would be unaware of being happy. Yet how many of us accept that our miseries are connected with the ability to feel happy and embrace them willingly? Furthermore, happiness is an ephemeral condition which phases in and out in varying degrees of intensity. So we might rephrase our life's wish as, 'I would like to be as happy as possible, as often as possible during my lifetime', while perhaps specifying conditions or circumstances which relate to our subjective ideas of happiness – such as health, wealth, being loved and so on.

(36)

Why don't we set aside a contrastive condition, such as happiness, and see if we can find a universal and unvarying concept to inform our lives. I suggest that a more appropriate goal is the search for meaning. I express this axiomatically as 'The meaning of life is the search for meaning'. This orientation will be able to make sense of contrastive and ephemeral states and to drain them of their significance. Treat everything you encounter, all situations, as your teacher and you can never stop being fascinated by your life. Even the state of boredom is interesting, if you look at it closely and ask what is really happening to you. Meaning is, in a sense, manufactured by the operation of awareness. It is a productive state, whereas in general we are trained to lapse into consumptive states, to be consumers rather than producers.

(37)

Various things must be balanced to live life to the optimum. A subject very much worth thinking about is energy. Like the air we breathe, energy tends to be a subject only thought about when it starts to be missed, when it wanes and has to be rationed and struggled after. A modern condition, long thought to be a psychosomatic illness, characterised by a debilitating lack of energy is Post Viral Fatigue Syndrome and there are many other conditions which, possibly, are a product of mismanaged energy leading to chronic imbalances and eventually illness. Which comes first, the low energy or the virus which, once established, sustains that condition?

(38)

It is not very sensible to ignore the effects of our environments, like coal miners refusing to wear respirators because they are uncomfortable. We work in offices and factories polluted chemically and electronically. We travel in tunnels filled with air unfit to breathe.

(39)

Whenever we do something we are either in 'production mode' or 'consumption mode'. I am not talking here of the physiological aspects or the metabolism of food, but of something more metaphysical. Two seemingly identical situations may be, in this sense, opposite in nature. One may be productive and the other consumptive. Telling them apart relies on the capacity to see real effects.

(40)

Consider the example of a dinner party where the guests have middle-class manners and mostly know each other. Perhaps there are one or two newcomers; the sexes evenly balanced. Typically, especially among the males, a mild struggle for domination will ensue. Like chickens thrown together for the first time, a pecking order must be established. The ways in which this takes place may vary and may involve civilised conversational strategies and gentility rather than crude aggression. But unless someone actively works to prevent it – and often this role falls to the women present – this tendency to establish hierarchies by competition operates like a default setting in a universal programme of behaviour.

This habit of behaviour is a problem, as it is inevitably geared to enabling the consumption of satisfactions. I say something witty and consume your enjoyment of the remark. The engagement of egos on these occasions is such that the chance of something *real* or *sincere* being communicated, a productive effect, is extremely remote. For a productive effort to come about – and this usually needs to be managed by someone who is both aware of its nature and knows how it can be provoked in any given set of circumstances (and the circumstances are based on right timing, the right gathering of people and the correct situation) – the sense of competing needs to be suspended. It must be established that no prizes or lemons will result from the exchanges. Everyone must *sincerely* hope to learn something *real*.

(41)

Each day a multitude flows through the Underground tunnels, yet everyone is separate. 'Only connect', says E. M. Forster; 'Only diverge', replies the urban crowd. We need to learn to take the risks of sharing. For social creatures, separation is a form of death.

(42)

No matter who you are, you have participated in a unique pattern of experiences in your life; if you share them with me, and perhaps I can add to them with experiences from my own life – and where it is kept in mind that experiences are not opinions, read or other-wise – then we may both enhance our knowledge. A result, a product, may be generated to our mutual benefit. We need each other for this and may in this way achieve something of a qualitatively different order from what could arise by acting alone.

(43)

Perhaps you believe that I am stating the obvious. That such exchanges are commonplace. In over a decade of watching for this kind of thing to arise *spontaneously*, I have noted it on only three occasions.

(44)

We might usefully look at the unspoken questions we all have at the back of our minds in our interactions with each other. A great deal of the underlying and generally hidden motivation for behaviour can be understood and explained by considering just two questions. The first, 'Do I exist?', leads into the second, 'Does my existence matter?'

We are continuously engaged on the task of confirming and enhancing our perception that our lives have existential meaning and value. Normally this takes the form of evaluating ourselves by comparisons. When unchecked by reflection this can easily turn into a tyrannical taskmaster: I am cleverer, more attractive, richer than you, and so have more substantial claim to the sense that I exist more significantly than you do and matter more. Certainly, my existence matters more for me than for anyone else, but this is a far cry from unconscious parlaying into 'therefore my existence is more meaningful than that of everyone else I meet'. And yet we all do this in whichever area of our self-image is easiest to market: brain, body, lifestyle, wealth.

(45)

The person who may seem to have low self-esteem is a person who may tend to answer these unconscious enquiries in the negative – and thereby feels like a ghost and matters hardly, if at all. This leads to a desire, almost a reflex, to assert oneself as a way to cancel this uneasy sense of not really existing.

(46)

Such self-doubts are good examples of the essential falsity of the constructed personality we must all occupy. This personality is largely an accidental composite which might even be thought of as a large dustbin into which a fairly random sequence of 'visitors' – actual people met in life, things read and observed – have dumped impressions. Some of these impressions have decayed to nothing and some have, like Styrofoam, resisted the composting effect and remain intact in the personality dustbin.

(47)

When we meet someone and interact with them, we stand next to our dustbin and poke around in it to show what it contains. It gives off a particular aroma, pleasant or foul according to the layer closest to the surface and additionally by reference to its overall content. The real self, the owner of the dustbin in my analogy, has but a shadowy existence and possesses a memory that he is not the contents of his dustbin. And yet the owner is compelled to display the dustbin's contents, failing to realise that a richer and more purposeful life exists *away from the bin*.

(48)

Personality dustbin display activity is not finally satisfying, any more than to show guests your discarded rubbish would be. It may indicate where you have been, what you have consumed, but it does not really show who you are. Some so-called self improvement systems and even religious methodologies operate on their adherents by enforcing a mechanism whereby the bin is gradually or even suddenly emptied. Unless they can also switch attention away from the compulsion of mutual bin-gazing, towards something more satisfying – ideally real communication between bin-owners – a crisis equivalent to 'my bin is empty, I do not exist', will follow. This leads to experienced nihilism, that there is no reality and the belief that we are nothing more than garbage. Remove that, and nothing remains. Unsurprisingly, this not in-frequently leads to mental collapse and an inability to function normally within ordinary societies.

(49)

Sincerity is the capacity to set aside such considerations, what I have heard referred to as an ego death! But it is really just a method to outmanoeuvre, for a limited time and a specific purpose, the bundle of conditioning which we think of as our personalities. We can stop performing and detach from expectation if we try and this puts us in touch with a deeper self, one which is sincere.

PART IV

Light at the End

If we see light at the end of the tunnel,
It's the light of the oncoming train.

'SINCE 1939', ROBERT LOWELL

Everything that goes into a saltmine becomes salt.

PROVERB

We do not ride on the railroad;
it rides upon us.

HENRY DAVID THOREAU

(1)

Suddenly alarm bells were ringing. Ringing with an insistent tone, like a child's cry, a noise designed to be impossible to ignore. Half way down Platform 6 I halted and listened carefully to the radio traffic. Listening would, I thought, provide the answers. There was no need to ask directly what we all wanted to know: *Was this for real? Was it just an exercise or a false alarm?*

(2)

Even indolent, resentful and surly SAs who daily special-ised in avoiding anything remotely resembling work were efficient and professional in evacuating the station in an emergency. It was a source of collective pride, always a team effort and a race against the clock. From the initial shock of the station alarm, to the metallic clash of the Boston Gates as they were pulled shut, it was regarded as a normal reaction time for the station to be emptied and closed in just three minutes. Anything slower was a cause for corporate shame. When the alarm bells rang, everyone ran about like clockwork wind-up toys magically turbo-charged, each knowing exactly where to go and what to do and doing it at the double.

(3)

This transformation, from a rabble of resentful workers suffering from an advanced case of the British disease, to an organic and efficient professional team, made me think of the army. In the downtime of a state of peace it was every man for himself, almost everyone would be hellbent on skiving until a real problem or genuine emergency presented itself and only then would unity materialise from nowhere. The enemy would be very professionally faced down, eliminated, without apparent effort and with a superabundance of *sang froid*, an attitude verging on boredom or the mechanicality of a well-oiled machine, as each task followed the one before with the automatic elegance of a dancer's inborn sense of rhythm.

But it didn't last. Once the station was emptied and then closed, the tight ship reverted to pre-emergency type and the surly mannerisms were resumed to deal with the flood of enquiries from the irritated would-be travellers now locked out of the system.

(4)

There were various reasons for deciding to close a station. Overcrowding occasionally. Fire always: following King's Cross no risks were ever taken. A suspect package which would not reveal its contents by examination at a distance. And the genuine suspected bomb whenever bomb-scare warnings had been issued by the police to the Underground management, a situation which sometimes seemed seasonal.

I knew a bomb warning had been given the previous week. Stations had been opening and closing day by day, like a nervous reflex or sequence of flinches anticipating a punch. Victoria and King's Cross mainline stations had been roped off by the bomb squad three times in the past two days. You could almost smell the cordite in the air, but this was my imagination running wild and Semtex has no smell.

(5)

I ran up to a cluster of people at the end of my platform. A woman was reading a novel, Louis de Bernières' *Captain Corelli's Mandolin*. It was the book of the moment. The wide variety of commuter texts you might expect, the hundreds of different interests which an 'everyone's different' assumption made likely, were nowhere visible. Just the same two or three books read by everyone who bothered to read at all. It was a small confirmation of our herd instinct. I got her attention and noticed how she kept her place in the book, dog-earing the page, finger and thumb moving automatically and not requiring the oversight of her conscious mind. Motioning to a middle-aged man reading a racing form and circling horses names and to two Suits staring at an advertising poster for Wonderbras, I rapidly explained in short, clipped sentences what was going on, adopting an urgent, no-bullshit tone.

'The station is closed. There are no trains. Please leave as quickly as you can by the nearest exit,' gesturing over my right shoulder at the exit sign a few feet behind where we were standing. 'Do not run, but be as quick as you can.'

'What's up?' asked the tipster, chewing the end of his pen, as if to concentrate on my reply.

'Bomb,' I answered, correcting myself after a moment, 'suspected bomb,' and as he and the others walked towards the escalators to the street added, 'No point gambling on everything.'

(6)

Sometimes I imagine myself dying. Death, in my imagination, always comes suddenly, unbidden and un-expectedly. Before dying I am, of course, doing some-thing. Mostly in these daydreams it is something especially ordinary: making a cup of coffee; cleaning my teeth; reading the newspaper. And always I can't help thinking – and knowing I am about to die – my last act!

Marcus Aurelius writes that you should try to do each thing as if it were your last act. Your epitaph. The one thing by which you will be remembered, the thing by which the world will judge you, everything else not noticed or somehow erased. It isn't easy to do this for very long. Try it! But I am haunted by the idea.

(7)

A friend recounts an embarrassing story. We are eating olives at my kitchen table as he talks. He tells me how he found his grandfather dead on the lavatory. He had to break down the locked door on receiving no answer to his repeated 'Are you all right?' And there was his grandfather, trousers around his ankles, dead.

I knew that the symptoms of a heart attack often seem like an attack of wind and that dying on the seat of ease was commonplace. My friend removed an olive pit from his mouth saying: 'He died as he lived, my granddad.' 'What do you mean?' I said. 'He didn't give a shit.'

(8)

I followed the departing group into the cross passages, nearly colliding with a middle-aged woman with a harassed expression. 'I can't find the Central Line,' she lamented, 'why are there no signs?' We were standing next to one, but to point this out would have been superfluous.

'It's closed,' I said. 'The Central Line is closed.' This wasn't the answer she wanted. 'Oh – my – God!' each word drawled, enunciated slowly and with a heavy emphasis on the last word. 'It's taken nearly an hour to get here. How long will I have to wait now? Why can't you improve the service? Call this a railway – and its so expensive!' At this she waved her season ticket under my nose to show me how much money she had spent to go nowhere and as if she was considering whether or not to throw the useless thing away.

I held up my hand to turn off her tirade. There was no time for this, I thought. 'Please listen. The station's closed. Just leave now. It's an emergency.' I pointed to the exit. She did not seem the sort of woman to tell about a bomb, so I didn't mention it. She obeyed, but I could tell she resented being told what to do by an employee of a failing and costly institution.

(9)

Yes, this was all taking too long. I mentally peeled off the outer leaves of habitual politeness, revealing a crisp green heart of practical necessity. Time to go up a gear. A minute had passed by my watch since the alarm was silenced and the PA announced its recorded message to clear the station. Two minutes left!

I turned into the long passageway and spotted two youths slinking along at a snail's pace. Each wore a Walkman, each was enclosed in a bubble of sound. I sprinted into their line of vision and madly waved for them to return to the here and now. 'Out now!' I ordered in my best taking-no-prisoners voice. 'Unless you want to die!' I added dramatically. The youths, in beanies and baggy everything, didn't seem to know if I was threatening to kill them on the spot or trying to save them from some unperceived danger. 'Now!' I repeated. 'It's a bomb and the station's closed.'

(10)

I was beginning to enjoy the drama and could feel reserves of energy, a surge of adrenaline, kicking in. My usual Maître d' courtesy could be safely set aside. Any degree of rudeness was sanctioned by the expediency of the emergency. It was invigorating to give orders. A rush. Is this what politicians feel like? Or generals? Circumstances mean that your authority must be obeyed, your orders acted upon at once, without debate.

'Out now! Leave the station *right now!*' I repeated at the diminishing number of stragglers I met on the way to the Central Line. My colleagues were no doubt busy doing the same, which is why there were so few people despite the rush-hour only just having drawn to a close. I had covered four of the six platforms in under two minutes. One minute to go . . . I told myself to move faster.

(11)

Tearing down Platform 1 I opened the Station Closed sign. The flashing light, which was used to signal to drivers, failed to flash when I threw the switch and I remembered that the battery was flat and that I had been asking for a new one for weeks. It didn't matter much as no trains would come through the station with a suspected bomb near the platform. I repeated this task on Platform 2 and, phoning in my progress on a nearby Autophone, learned from Old Tom, the Supervisor in the Control Room, that the 'bomb', although it was safer to think of it as THE BOMB, was in the cross passages about twenty feet from where I was now standing. This was not a good place to be. Should it explode at this moment. Or the next moment or a few moments after the next moment . . .

(12)

When I was fourteen I had been jolted out of the cinema seat I was occupying by a force like an earthquake. The public house next to the cinema had just exploded. Another bomb in another nearby pub blew up a few minutes later. I followed the frightened and dazed crowd into a hellish street scene. Men and women were staggering around bleeding, the women mostly crying, many holding their hands over their ears. Blood ran down several faces. Some of the men – one a taxi driver, perhaps the driver of the cab lying on its side a few feet from where I was standing – were helping the injured to move further along the street away from the pub doorway which was streaming black smoke like a ship's funnel. The police and ambulances were beginning to arrive. Then the sirens of five fire engines converged like the music in a round.

I was shepherded away behind a yellow tape with the word Police repeated every few feet in large blue letters. I watched transfixed by the scenes of carnage. Nothing so dramatic had happened to me before. The firemen were carrying blankets as stretchers, but they seemed to be too light to contain bodies. Later I learned that they had been carrying away arms and legs, bits and pieces of the victims, detached by the bomb blast and now awaiting identification.

In my twenties I went to Harrods to buy a tie. I needed a new tie and although I did not usually shop at this famous London landmark, I thought it would be fun to do so on this occasion. It was sunny and I watched children sail their boats on the round pond in Kensington Gardens before walking to the Knightsbridge store. When I was nearly there I found the surrounding streets a no-go area. There had been a bomb, explained a policewoman. It had exploded in the menswear department.

In my early thirties, visiting a friend living in Karachi who worked as an engineer redesigning trucks for the Pakistani military, I decided to while away some time by seeing a movie. A random exploration of the cinemas in the downtown area which I had looked over the day before yielded nothing of outstanding interest. But I wondered about a film in Pukhtu – the local variant of the Afghani language Pushto. I spoke Farsi and hoped I would be able to manage without too much of a struggle.

Inside the cinema were the usual assortment of daytime men and boys with nothing to do, all of whom were gnawing their way through huge bags of sunflower seeds; the cinema floor was carpeted with spent husks. The film started and I watched for about fifteen minutes before realising that Pukhto was not Persian and I had no idea what was going on – and found I didn't care.

Leaving the cinema I hailed a passing tonga. Ten minutes after I had given up on the film and left, I calculated the next day while reading the front-page story in the morning paper, the cinema exploded. Five dead, sixteen seriously injured.

I will soon be forty.

(13)

It only took a second to imagine what could happen. Fragments of concrete and metal – the plaster on the platforms was fixed over a grill of wire, like chickenwire, and any explosion would immediately convert this material into shrapnel, superheated segments of wire that would julienne strip anyone caught in the blast – rushing towards you at hundreds of feet per second. The words 'The confined space massively magnified the explosion,' in the voice of a TV newsreader came into my mind. The voice continued, 'The bodies have not yet been identified . . .' No, I thought. There wouldn't be much to identify and my dental records would be impossible to find as my active dislike of dentists had kept me away from them for over twenty years.

I didn't want to die on Platform 1, among the grime of the Central Line, vaporised for pocket money doing a job no one appreciated. How much pause did we ever give to consider staff killed in some public disaster? I remembered that the Sarin nerve gas attack in Tokyo had killed at least one member of the subway staff who had heroically helped to carry a dying passenger out of the station. I could not remember his name, doubted that anyone could, except his family and friends. There was no significance in such a death. Hero was a label we would apply to comfort ourselves at the futility of a death on the job. No job description included 'dying, if absolutely necessary', except perhaps soldier or body-guard and these days even these martial professions were being redefined to exclude this. Certainly, it was my duty to do what I could to clear the station, warn the innocent. In the three minutes it took I would earn nearly 40p. Less than the price of a Mars Bar. Was that, then, the price of my life in the situation I had volun-tarily got myself into?

(14)

I was, however, protected by a thick wall of assumption. I assumed I would not die in the next few seconds, that the click-delete of God's mouse on my name and existence would not yet occur. It was an assumption I made each day, that we all make. There was no debate about the reasonableness of risking my life for 40p – and this was not what was happening. I was simply doing what was necessary without regard for the conse-quences as there was no means for me reasonably to evaluate the real risk. And there was no time. Don't think, just move faster, seemed like a good plan. Act first, panic later.

(15)

I belted up the escalators. Someone had reversed all the down escalators so that they went up, like a Get Out of the Underworld card. Everything now led up, to the open air, to the outside, to safety, away from the immediate threat of obliteration.

I crossed the Bullring and made for the RVP exit, the point where we rendezvous-ed, and were counted off on a clipboarded list of names to confirm no one had been forgotten and left behind, that no one was locked in. That all were present and accounted for.

(16)

As this was a suspected bomb we were, in theory, required to regroup at the secondary RVP in front of All Souls church a couple of hundred yards further along Upper Regent Street. I looked through the streaming sunlight at the outline of the church spire in the distance and wondered if it was by Nicholas Hawksmoor. But as the area around the entrances to the station had not yet been roped off, and the bomb squad had yet to arrive, it seemed a cowardly thing to do. Members of the public were still milling around trying to get into the station, and so, standing at the drawn gates, the knowing and those ignorant of the danger relied on the hundred feet of concrete between us and THE BOMB to keep us safe.

(17)

The echoing sirens, which seemed to be coming from all four points of the compass, resolved into two blue transit vans, lights flashing, and three smaller police vehicles racing up Regent Street. Cars and taxis pulled over to let them through. One of the vans slid to a halt near where I was standing. The DSM and two Supervisors walked over to brief the bomb squaddies, clutching the station plan, a large paper diagram flapping in the light breeze. Three officers in body armour and helmets with neck flaps and visors struggled to carry a large trunk into the station. I wondered what was inside – anti-bomb paraphernalia? A medical kit? They looked like beetles, the shiny blue-black of their body armour, oily, briefly reflecting a rainbow of colours as one man passed me, and reinforcing the idea of a beetle's carapace or wing-case. Insects burrowing underground, I thought, as they, men who risked their lives for a living, disappeared, one by one, below.

(18)

All things one has forgotten scream for help in dreams.
ELIAS CANETTI

Now it is night and I am in my small bedroom, at the top of the house, sleeping. It is not an easy slumber and I turn over, twisting and changing positions without waking. Perhaps I moan, or speak incoherently. No one coming into that room at that time would easily be able to guess what I am experiencing.

(19)

I run through the tunnels shouting at the thousands of people swarming along, each intent on his or her thoughts, lost to the world around them, separately enclosed. Rank upon rank of faces surge forward like waves in a human sea. I shout at them, but there is no sound. I wave my arms to attract the attention of the group closest to me. They do not see me, do not hear me. In fact, they walk right through me – and then, only then, do I realise I am a ghost, insubstantial, not real to them, beyond any sense register they can experience or credit as existing.

I can feel a terrible urgency. I must warn, yet at the same time know my warnings – about an imminent but non-specific disaster – will not be heeded. How could they be? No one can hear me. No one can see me. I can feel my heart pounding faster as I come to understand this.

I know I must empty the tunnels. Something terrible is about to happen. I cannot remember what it is; I know what it is but have forgotten. This lapse in memory increases the sense of panic. I can feel runnels of sweat sliding down my face as I dash from one part of the station to another. I must move faster.

A woman is laughing as she listens to a remark passed by her male companion. She seems ridiculous to me, laughing, amusing herself instead of doing what she should do. I stand and watch the couple walk towards Platform 2. I know there is now no more time for anything. 'It is time,' I say to myself in confirmation of this thought. And at once, immediately, feel a rush of air. There is a flash, heat and light at the same time.

(20)

I wake and sit up, heart pounding, too hot, breathing audibly.

Just a dream, I realise. The mind discharging the unexpired emotions of the day. Nothing for it but to go back to sleep, and in the morning to carry on where I left off.